NATASHA DIONNE

BEAUTIFUL POWERFUL YOU
Journey In - To The Voice Of Your Soul

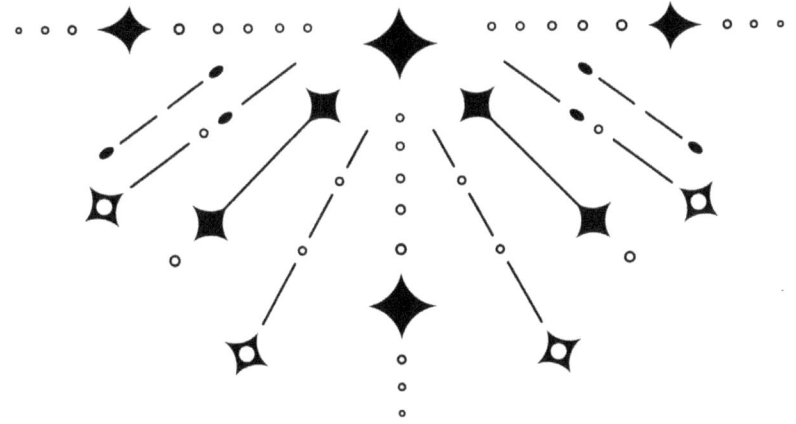

Beautiful Powerful You: Journey In – To The Voice Of Your Soul
© Natasha Dionne 2022

www.natasha-dionne.com

The moral rights of Natasha Dionne to be identified as the author of this work have been asserted in accordance with the Copyright Act 1968.

First published in Australia 2022 by Natasha Dionne

ISBN 978-0-6452668-0-1

Any opinions expressed in this work are exclusively those of the author and are not necessarily the views held or endorsed by Natasha Dionne.

All rights reserved. No part of this publication may be reproduced or transmitted by any means, electronic, photocopying or otherwise, without prior written permission of the author.

Disclaimer

All the information, techniques, skills and concepts contained within this publication are of the nature of general comment only, and are not in any way recommended as individual advice. The intent is to offer a variety of information to provide a wider range of choices now and in the future, recognising that we all have widely diverse circumstances and viewpoints. Should any reader choose to make use of the information herein, this is their decision, and the author and publisher/s do not assume any responsibilities whatsoever under any conditions or circumstances. The author does not take responsibility for the business, financial, personal or other success, results or fulfilment upon the readers' decision to use this information. It is recommended that the reader obtain their own independent advice.

Dedicated to...

My kidliwinks, Taegan & Chad. To your sacred, soul-driven creative and inspired futures and for the endless love and magic you gift me for being your mum. I love you two sho mush! xxx

Aunty Sandy & Uncle Al, for your enduring support and unwavering love for me and all that has come through me, including my babies, lol. I love you two gazillions xxx

Mum and Dad.

Mum, for bringing me to life and not terminating me. Phew! Thank you for accepting me, however you find me today. I love you loads xxx

Dad, for adopting 2 year old me when you married Mum, and for your desire to heal the past with love and connection. Thank you for trying so hard to keep us close. I miss loving you xxx

My beautiful friends, Jacki, Dannie and Suz, for being fans of my healings and writings, even when I was just raving about showing up and sharing more. Thank you for your patience and trust in me. You are treasured gems xxx

Aunty Tabby, my soul sister, for your deep loving care and conscious connection, over all of the years we have been related...and not, haha! I love you Honeypuff xxx

My brother, Damon, for your encouragement to share my writings with the world back in 2008 when I hadn't realised the depth of what was going on here...yet! You took an instant interest and valued what I was receiving. I love you for that and more xxx

My brothers and sister, nieces, nephews, cousins, extended family, blended family, friends and the whole of humanity.

No matter where you feel you are in your journey, I see you, and I'd love to hear from you. I hope you find the courage to reach out and play in the fields of energy and emotion that surround you, with me, with someone else, someone special, someone who honours you and cares about your wellbeing at their core.

I give the intent that this book finds its little way of bringing more of us together in harmony. From my humble human being and my touchy-feely soul, this is for you. This is me. 😊

Thank you for reading this far. I love you xxx
Natasha

Goddess

One Spring sunrise many moons ago, another beautiful goddess was born. She did not know that she was a goddess. In fact, she thought that she was almost invisible and that no one would ever notice her. As she grew up, the goddess learned to love life and gave her energy to others wherever she could. Everyone loved the goddess, even though she did not know it or feel it.

One day, the goddess awoke to the sensation of her shadow. The goddess's shadow showed her a mirror, at which the goddess burst into tears, for the goddess suddenly realised that she was totally visible and had been all the time. The goddess discovered many aspects of herself as she reflected upon her being, in every mirror.

Without judgment or blame, the goddess acknowledged, accepted and worked on integrating every one of these aspects along with many other attributes to fulfill her inner desire to be conscious and whole. Fearless and empowered, the goddess learned to live and love in a different light. Following her inner wisdom, the goddess chose to shine her light on others, and encouraged them to do the same. The goddess thanked her shadow for bringing truth into her life and promised to love and nurture herself for the beautiful, powerful goddess she was, happily and infinitely after.

What if God... was... one of us?.... (or all of us?)

– Joan Osborne

Table of Contents

Introduction 1

1 – Me, Myself & I 12

2 – Energy Of Love 20

3 – Human Illusions 26

4 – Give Your Heart Wings 38

5 – G.O.D 46

6 – Intuitive 54

7 – Ego 64

8 – Guiding Light 76

9 – Let Go 86

10 – The World Is Your Oyster 102

11 – Flying High 114

12 – Depression 122

13 – Kundalini 130

14 – Winds Of Change 144

15 – Time To Come Out 152

16 – Transformation 160

Table of Contents

17 – Clearing Pain 168

18 – Windows To The Soul 174

19 – Wireless Beings 188

20 – Happy Anniversary 198

21 – Self Love 214

22 – Wish You Were Here 220

Conclusion 231

Acknowledgements 234

About The Author 237

Love Note 238

Introduction

Due to my unusual experiences as a child, I was afraid of the dark. I was scared I would bump into the beings that I could sense or see in my mind's eye before the lights went out. Unable to make sense of my inter-dimensional connections, I constantly feared what we then called 'Ghosts' and 'Aliens'.

Nae Nae NZ, 1970's

I was a sensitive child, unbalanced and unfocused. I was called a 'dreamer' because I was always 'away with the fairies'. I struggled to be present, sit still, listen or participate logically and practically due to internal and multidimensional experiences that I doubted anyone around me would comprehend any more than I could. I went through stages of struggle to get words out of my mouth with ease, and that also made sense. Still, I managed to attract my nickname, Tasha 2ZB, after a local radio station because I talked a lot (too much?)

Waking to a wet bed was a regular occurrence, and I felt terribly ashamed. If I needed the toilet at night, I would visualise the floor next to my bed where I would put my feet, but all I could see was a mass of webs and spiders occupying that space. This added to my fright, and there was no way in heck I was going to attempt to put a foot out of my blankets in case they were real. I kept telling myself that they couldn't be real, but their creepiness had me shaking further into fear.

These were no incey, wincey spiders!

Then, there were the visions of several wolves viciously jumping up the back of the house where the little sunroom I slept in looked out to. It was all in my mind's eye, but it was terrifying not knowing what would happen next. What was all this about? Why was I seeing all this scary non-sense? Perhaps these realities were merely symbolic of fear itself, the energy of my own and the collectives showing up as a holographic picture show. The Universe speaks to us in many ways. How we interpret signs and symbols shapes our reality. Goodness knows what I was supposed to do with all that imagery as a human child at that time. How many adults would have been readily available to help me ask my own body of wisdom the right questions to decipher, deconstruct, dissolve and deal with my multi-layered, dimensional dilemmas?

Every night when I went into my bedroom to sleep, I could feel energies, the presence of unexplained phenomena.

I could hear whispers and feel my skin crawling with a mixture of energy that I would describe as fear-filled, and desperate. I felt like I was about to be eaten alive. Perhaps I was feeling the hidden reality of my own restlessness, insecurities and a hard-to-love existence, with the support of invisible help that had trouble getting through to me. This presence did not have a physical body but many energy bodies instead. Sometimes it was as if every embodied soul before me that had been tortured or died unjustly were hovering in my room, screaming for me to acknowledge them so they could communicate their messages of confusion, hurt and frustration too.

I was later faced with these energies and entities, learning to relieve them of their pains and move them on willingly. Other times, my room would be lit with flashing red and blue lights, and I would be beckoned to far away places by familiar and powerful beings who would not take 'no' for an answer. Instead of reaching out to them, I withdrew, scared I would go too far and be unable to find my way back home. I held every muscle in my body so tight that I could barely support the shallow breath I would allow myself in order to avoid any encounter that I thought I could die from. At the peak of my fear, my small body would shake uncontrollably and then suddenly become paralyzed until one of two things happened:

*I would sense and clairvoyantly see the palm of a hand moving towards me and gently touch my shoulder, at which point I would feel a slight sense of relief as the energies in the room dispersed and let me be. I desperately anticipated this outcome every night in the hope that I would be left alone to sleep somewhat peacefully.

OR

* I would feel a presence beside me and a gentle voice whisper 'shhhh, it's okay'.

And then,

* I would feel myself leaving my body, reluctantly being stretched and pulled through my chest and leaping at the same time, for fear of being stuck in no woman's land. I guess this was when my body rested, and my spirit was free to roam in a space of weightlessness, bizarre adventures, expansion and the matrix of possible, concurrent lives. Lives outside my third-dimensional reality that made it confusing and excruciating to return to the entrapment of my tiny and vulnerable human body.

In the midst of these experiences, I would attempt to alert my parents of my discomfort by screaming, but my voice would freeze. My throat burned with pain, under the pressure of my shrilling, though silent, screams, as I found myself surrounded by the fear and uncertainty of troubled strangers and unwanted visitors and then left to deal with them on my own. With a tight knot in my stomach, I would lay in the fetal position, rubbing my ankles together until I could no longer feel them. I broke through the skin sometimes, and once, on my 5th birthday, I tore a pair of socks I was gifted with and loved so much that I just had to wear them to bed too. I was shocked and couldn't understand how I had ruined my new socks. I also worried I would get into trouble in the morning for being careless and rough and not being able to explain how or why.

I have shorter teeth on one side of my mouth still from grinding my teeth incessantly, even by day, wishing and hoping that someone would help me out of this unexplainable mess. My teeth grinding did not stop until my late 30's as I consciously worked on calming my anxieties and felt safe enough to sleep without worry of energetic interference. I never felt relaxed. Even when I closed my eyes, I could see stuff. It was as if my eyes never closed at all as there was always a picture of another reality that demanded my attention. My clairvoyance was heightened and harassed me constantly as I watched movie-style visions play out in my first eye area between the brows. ChrisTian Ra taught me the third eye is actually the first eye and that feels right for me too.

This state of being strained my eyes as I desperately attempted to close them tighter until the visions disappeared. They did not go away in a hurry, so I was regularly exhausted of my energy to function easily and well. The scare factor was so intense that it overwhelmed me. I found it impossible to communicate my night-time terrors to anyone. I'm not sure how it would have been received or understood had I managed to spit anything out. Hmmm? Guess we will never know. I felt tremendously cursed for years and worried that it would never end. I struggled to keep my awareness in my small body during the day.

Because I could not express my inner turmoil, I found myself fearing almost everything that felt uneasy. I preferred to hide outside of myself as if I wasn't really there. Lights were on, but no one was home.

Interestingly, it was during my sleep that the freeze on my bedtime voice eventually lifted. This was when we had moved from Nae Nae to Wainuiomata. The only people that woke were my shocked and light sleeping parents. I did not snap out of my sleep state. I would just sit bolt upright, yell profanity and then lay back down as if nothing had happened. Loud, shrieking fudge bombs, capable of waking the deaf, screamed through the house. Eeeek! My dad would apparently run to my rescue, only to find no obvious intrusion. Sorry Dad xxx

By day I regularly found myself entering a void. I would suddenly and involuntarily find myself totally expanded beyond my body, feeling separated from it and unable to see it or feel its density at all. My fear of uncertainty and lack of comprehension challenged my breathing. I could not feel breath entering my invisible body. I struggled to understand my experiences. My way to cope eventually came as I witnessed a new perspective. I sensed that my being was nestled amongst the clouds in the sky, yet clouded in nothingness at the same time. Much like being snow-blind, I was blended and camouflaged within my environment, unable to get my bearings. All I could do was observe invisible energy and breath, clairvoyantly, as if tiny little me was actually part of an entire, omnipresent Universe. These experiences frightened and controlled me.

I was scared I had disappeared off the face of the Earth, without a trace, unable to speak out loud for anyone to hear and notice, unaware of how to make my way back to the safety of my protective human body. I worried profusely that I might abandon my Earth family for good, leaving them immersed in an unexplained tragedy, causing endless havoc in their heads and grief in their hearts. I did not like it there. There were no answers for me at this time, nor any adequate questions to satisfy my curiosities or insecurities. Nothing was available to settle my fragile nervous system. Only a huge invisible hole in creation that sucked me up, held me in and spat me out at its will. I felt ill-equipped to explain any of this. Thankfully, I was always eventually shocked back into my body…until next time!

A beautiful, powerful experience

On the nights my room was filled with flashing blue and red lights, I would feel extreme cold on my energy body as I left my vulnerable human incarnation to zoom around the solar system amongst the stars in a mass of light and energy. I was not always supported by a vehicle and would sometimes find myself transported to a place I would now call 'The Healing Room'. This room had a sense of tranquillity and serenity like nothing else I have encountered. Its boundaries appeared as white walls of light, suspended in a gentle pocket of weightlessness.

The atmosphere was slightly hazy and magical, with long strips of luminous, transparent streamers hanging from high above and continuing far below me. There was no visible floor. I did not need one. I just floated in and across the tables of light that appeared like holographic yoga mats levitating in stillness until I felt ready to settle over one. I did not feel my dense physical frame in this private cosmic space, only my deep, airy and expanded energy body of self. As I hovered mid-air, a subtle sense of fullness and emptiness seemed to merge within me and then my awareness would disappear completely until the morning.

I was always calm and alone here. I had, however, sensed other light beings that provided and monitored this dreamy sanctuary anonymously, as if standing behind a two-way mirror, just out of plain sight. A delicate sound and vibration resonated throughout this domain, relaxing my spirit and giving me hope for love and understanding to greater proportions than I knew existed. This experience was like a rejuvenating vacation, gifting my being with a bliss-filled sensation. I did not need to lie down to feel it. Although this particular adventure was not scary for me, I could not fathom how or why it was happening, nor could I control it.

Get to know... the feeling... of liberation....and relief
– Crowded House

Introduction

I was not usually a fan of participating in anything involuntary. I stood solidly by my will and choice and rebelled against almost everything else that came my way. Returning to my Earth-side home and waking up in my dependent form each morning created great stress and confusion for many years. It was a feeling of extreme discomfort, like being trapped in an area too small to breathe, move and feel joy in. I eventually came to realise why the human journey is a constant work in progress. We are much more than we know and we are settling for much less than our beautiful, powerful souls have the ability to create and be, even while playing in this dense version of reality.

This was not the end of my strange and variable experiences. When the poems started coming through to me in my late 30's, it was the beginning of a new chapter of self discovery, acceptance and care. I learned there were versions of me in a multitude of dimensional realities that I would tap into by using all of my senses. This includes the subtle senses that can tune into and play with high ranging frequency and galactic experience. This was a chapter I could not speed through or gloss over. It was a weird and wonderful time for me as I celebrated and grieved through the personal transformation process. Then I moved with my small family from New Zealand to Australia. Though I sit alone at home and write, I am aware that I am not alone in my experience. The time has come to open up and share for the benefit of others who sit in silence and fear of unfathomable happenings. I feel for the kiddies that can't sleep at night. Those who are unable to learn through the day or live up to certain adult expectations. I wonder how many of them have impossible tasks trying to work out what this life is all about.

>>>>

I am writing this book because it is within me pleading to be expressed and heard. I like to think it will help my children understand their mum better. How she was in her lifetime, her deep thoughts, feelings, experiences, insights, behaviours, choices and why's. I give the intent that it helps them continue the healing of energy around family lineage, traumas, tragedies and disconnection. Perhaps it may reopen the ancestral lines of communication that would love some tender loving care and begin a new family story for you too. I would love to have a story of my parents' lives, including my unknown birth father. I'm curious how they would tell their own life stories so that we may celebrate them for all they are or were. Our family could learn more about our similarities and differences and how human, being, went for them. I feel this would strengthen ongoing generational awareness and support. **Just putting it out there!**

My intent is to provide awareness around suffering and how to resolve and restore harmony, by connecting the experiences of our marvellous minds, beautiful bodies and powerful souls. By recognizing similarities and sharing differences, I believe we can each make an impact on Humanity's collective life experience and keep our beautiful, powerful planet and personal energy fields spinning happily and well.

I am a storyteller. I love to tell stories about our abilities to expand and transform beyond our mind's limited comprehension of multiple realities. I love to explore ways of removing constricting barriers to the depth of our heart energy. I would love this book to be the instigator of many a chitchat and inspire greater connection and joy amongst the vast similarities and differences of each human soul experience, with hearts wide open. My stories tell how I perceived my own journey and how I managed my own energy input and output. How I dealt with private hurts and released myself from continued intangible suffering. I give the intent that you will relate these stories to your own truth and find the healing and acceptance your soul desires for you too. May your path be fuelled with love and be driven by magic, consciousness and joy, always.

Natasha xxx

1 – Me, Myself & I

Me, myself, I, shadows and all
Spiralling into life on Earth, dirty boots 'n' all
Black, white, grey shadows dim my light
Re-facing past conflictions, freeze, fight, flight
On our way to this dimension, the ball is crystal clear
Reducing newborn vision, it's fogged when we near

I really need my time and space
Can't deny my angry face
From the first puff of breath to the physical death
The mission's to clear up the previous wrath
Driven by ego, the insatiable mind
Quietly detrimental to all human-kind

We hit a brick wall that causes confusion
Which leads to the road of our own evolution
On this road, we have choices and unlimited potential
No need for impressive or fancy credentials
All we need here is love, for ourselves and others
Blended kin, soul sisters and brothers

For all life on Earth, all beings of light
Irrespective of race, privilege or right
We each need true love, to give and receive
If we practice our Mastery, it can be achieved
The first step to start with ourselves may be hard
If our hearts have been battered, bruised and bares scars

You may then reap many intangible rewards
And so, on the journey back home, head towards
Be assured that this process, no matter how slow
Will help you learn, to change and to grow
You are not on your journey alone here, my friend
We're all here beside you, to evolve and transcend
Let's do it together. Let's gain inner strength
On our travels through life, no matter the length

Saving Humanity

When I was a child, my dad would watch the six o clock news every night. It was full of sadness, fighting and fear. It scared me to no end, and I wondered if I would survive long enough to feel pleasure in my body without the constant emotions of worry forcing me to stay in flight mode. School didn't help either. At primary, we had to come to class with a piece of information around a current affair. I hated that with a vengeance. That alone caused my tummy to tighten and riddle me with anxiety. I saw so much sadness and trauma on that T.V. that I vowed to help restore justice to the good people one day.

I would be a Police Woman, an Armed Offender to be exact, so that I could protect the goodies from the baddies. I'd take them out with my weapon and keep the community safe. I would put a stop to the causes and causers of so much pain and suffering. All this going on in my childhood head just waiting to blow. It didn't blow straight away. It took years to build up, years of fear and worry of this crazy human world, on top of my nighttime terrors of dimensions less visible and spoken about. I have come to learn that the six o'clock news is not on my list of things to live for, nor is it something I wish to live my life by. It seems I was temporarily blinded by the shadows of time, gaming unfairly and using trickery to program humanity through tele-vision.

My insides were in knots, destroying my ability to relax and function happily. Thanks to a book my family had on the shelf about unusual stories and mysterious happenings, I developed a huge fascination with spontaneous human combustion. I wondered if the extreme feelings of being trapped between resistance and expression would qualify me for this disastrous phenomenon too. I wondered what had caused the fate of these precious souls and if there were any similar signs, anything I could recognise in my own experience. I wondered where these people just disappeared to, how it affected their families lives, and if I too would end up blown to smithereens if I wasn't careful or kind. When I began to have random out-of-body experiences during the day, I wondered if I had, in fact, been combusted into oblivion and unchained myself from my human body, once and for all. **Holy Universe!**

The world was moving...she was... right there with it...and she was – Talking Heads

Soul Message

Each hue-man light being comes with a range of dark, unexplored pockets of self. These pockets are not attached or detached exactly but connect, reflect and emanate many aspects of unique source energy and all distortions of the individual human experience. You call these shady pockets into one, labelling them, the shadow. Your shadow is the grey area that wishes to transit from the unknown into the light of your awareness, for acceptance and either letting in, or letting out. It is where the as yet unexpressed, uncertain, unexplained and unacceptable parts of yourself begin to shift out of complete hiding in preparation to be seen fully for what they are. They sit on the edge of your consciousness, looking for the safety, comfort and love that your high, lighted self has to offer. These attributes wait patiently for you to recognise, respect, accept and integrate them for a lighter expression. There is no time in this space, just a divine order in which you realign with unexplored dimensions of your self from all subsequent levels of possible reality.

You may feel like the shadow is holding you to ransom, throwing you under the bus or trying to extort all your dark secrets out into the open without caution or care. You can feel the shadows presence being resisted, where the energy of your perceptions, guilt, shame, obligations, burdens, sadness, responsibilities, commitments and expectations conflict with the energy of your desires, dreams, beliefs, values, wants, needs, happiness and current sources of joy. This experience of owning all of who you are, need only be a private event and will endeavour to be so when you provide the space for its timely release. You will be guided intuitively. Follow the signs before it hits you like a sucker punch... **Watch out!**

Sounds harsh, however, its purpose is for your own health and well-being. It is the journey of your own soul to piece together all aspects of yourself for a more whole-some human experience. You see, the shadow wants you to reconcile your guilt, shame, sadness and so on. It wishes to redeem your wholeness by making peace with your dark secrets, guilty pleasures and idiosyncrasies. It purely proposes that you welcome it as a part of you rather than something outside of you to avoid, isolate, segregate and run from.

The shadow is your channel, a passage for all that is right and good for you to pass through and manifest into your physical reality. Still your body, quiet your mind, calm your emotions and nervous system. Here you will likely face your shadow. **Guts and glory!**

Together you can dilute the heavy, stagnant energies that weigh you down. It is impossible to ditch parts of yourself that you are afraid of and attempt to disown. Instead, give them your attention, your silent word for resolve, your blessing to be heard and be. Recognise they are not exactly you. However, They are old or frequently absent parts of you that you have not named, tamed, forgiven or felt connected to yet. They are memories of painful truths and mistruths. They are unhealed experiences projected into the non-existent future. Sit with the energy of these parts, memories and possibilities circling you, even screaming through you and observe.

Allow their wisdom to enlighten you. Hear them out. Stare them out with kindness and inner standing. Your family tree may have gifted you with the energy of unhealed roots too. All efforts to help them will be felt forward and back. Do not shut them out, for they will keep knocking and rocking for inclusion over delusion.

2 – Energy Of Love

When the energy of love creeps up from your soul
Your heart slowly melts, and suddenly, you're whole
Energetically honoured, caressed and kissed
A sense of euphoria not to be missed

Time ticks by without you knowing
Your true self steps foremost, core energy glowing
It's magically dreamy, you're naturally high
Attracting abundance, no need to try

With answers before you as clear as blue sky
All has been given. No need to ask why
You're relaxed, enlightened, fulfilled and content
At peace with your journey and all you have spent

The Old School Yard

I rarely felt comfortable in the classroom. I was too afraid to put my hand up to go to the toilet, ask questions or participate consciously. What brought me joy was the time before the first bell went. My shoes were kicked off straight away, and the merriment began! Kids ran everywhere, frantically collecting freshly cut, green as (Kiwi term) grass the ride-on mower had left us to play with, **yay!**

Giant eggs and nests were in the making with all the cuttings. Screams of excitement filled the air as us girls strategically planned how we would steal the boys' stash of clippings to add to our own. The sweet-scented dew on the freshly cut lawn drove us into a state of euphoria, a dreamily contagious atmosphere and a magical feeling of being high on nature's delights alone. Nothing felt better than this. **Hmmmm, take me back!**

Interschool sports, Hangi's and Maori Performing Arts were also easy-peasy places to feel comfort and a sense of belonging in. Fun and laughter were the names of these games, and I was in, mind, body and soul. Connection was welcomed and encouraged. Everyone was friendly and happy.

My greatest love at little kids' school, though, was being chased by the boys. They would play 'tug of war' over me with the girls. When the boys won, my favourite boyfriend would sit on my belly, pin my wrists to the ground and plant sloppy kisses all over my face. He had my full presence and consent. I loved it! When the energy of love had worked its magic, I would wriggle free, squealing with laughter and ecstasy, and feeling totally desirable and loved. My plain-Jane opinion of myself backed back enough for me to feel another's truth.

And that's where my chase for love outside of myself began... and continued. **Oh ohh**! On this trail, I did not learn to say no in a hurry either.

Any love is good love (right?)...*so I took what I could get...mmmm* - Bachman Turner Overdrive

I wonder if missing out on this kind of spontaneous freedom to share love so naturally, would stifle our courage to reach out even more, to test the waters in all areas of our lives. Would it keep us afraid of rejection and failure to live up to certain ideals. Would it leave our dreams and relationships doomed from the start? I loved this innocence that once enveloped my young heart. May it live on, within me forever. Yesss!!

Love meee.... tendeer...love mee... true – Thank you, Elvis, *I'm still talking!*

Soul Message

Yes, I hear you! Love is not just for the young at heart, and the freedom to explore love in all forms is a force to be reckoned with. You are one of the lucky ones. You have experienced many sides to love and now have more opportunities to explore even deeper layers of love. Love in dimensions that do not hold the same needs of reciprocation, physical touch, matching apples with apples or any form of measurement or comparison. This is not love, for love's sake. This love is tainted with conditions in the hope of restoring self-worthiness and fulfilling neediness, an impossible task from this state of unawareness.

You have been a player in this game of love for all life, do not stop here. Put your heart into more of what you think, feel, say and do each day. Include yourself in this right and ritual of unconditional giving. Give to others from a space of respect and reverence only because you can, and you want to. Give love without expectation of receiving anything in return. Love is not a transaction. Put your heart into your soul's hands. Have faith in your ability to expand and attract love in ways that you have not yet recognised as such. Do not distract yourself from loving attention and intentions or attempt to extract love from anything or anyone. Love will find you and fill you up with peace and pleasure at the same pace as you become it. We are not talking about the obvious states of love that humans find themselves deep in the shallow end of. We are talking about higher levels of consciously included states of awareness, where loving energy deeply emits to and from all personal experience and through all expression.

Me – Okey Dokey!

I...Love to love you baby! – Donna Summer

3 – Human Illusions

Breaking the dance of human illusions
Comes with its upsets, its downs and confusions
The ego heats up, the soul cools us down
As we calibrate new energy and recon' fresh ground
Exploring dark shallows, dipping our toes
Feeling our gut, following its knows

Letting the mind... wander and go
Creating new paradigms, expansion and growth
Recharging energy as we consciously row
On the river of life where ebbs align flow
Paying the price of wisdom on ice
Til we share it with warmth, judgement-free

Biting our tongue and swallowing pride
As we choose love whole-istically
Adjusting our response ability
Owning experience, unconditionally
Accepting our mirrors, beauty and beast
Celebrating behaviours, alive and deceased

Embracing similarities and differences to
Your authentic and beautiful powerful you
Capturing joy, dishing it out
Shining a light, releasing all doubt
Searching for truth, doing the work
Bravely diving where skeletons lurk

Loving yourself, up and down
Honouring your temple, feet to crown
Treasuring the people and wisdom love brings
Nurturing hearts, to beat in full swing
Cradling your babies, whispering sweet somethings
Watching wishes unfold, giving full blessings

If you'd like to connect with your spiritual crew
Stand up and be counted. Follow it through
Be merry and light, hum, strum and play
Open new doors, skip through them, don't stray
Know thyself, best friend and worst foe
Welcome them in, for all they forgo

Could you be the change that you wish to see?
Will you clear the fog or hide in the trees?
Magnify spirits' divining light
Guiding one's soul, where presence meets might
The cup of life is in your hands
Watered fully upon your commands

On Earth, you're connected, magnetically so
Form quality connections, illuminate, glow
Beauty and power, in hands and feet
Step to your music, your magic, our treat
Inner strength real, wild and untamed
Weakened by labels that humans have named

Your journey through life, a drag, race or prize
Seeing through physical or intuitive eyes
Is your energy stagnant or can you feel shifts?
Explore and embody, your talents, your gifts
Is your mind filled with focused, constructive chatter?
Does it rattle and roll with unruly natter?

Head down and chin up with heart on your sleeve
Feeling your way through all you perceive
Chaos, catastrophe, distress and strife
Slicing through ego, a double-edge knife
It's all about love, no drama, no fluff
Best given and received when clear with your 'stuff'

It's up to you to unpack your bags
Insecurities and lack stand out like red rags
Go in, bring them out, lighten your load
May the fireworks inside you expire, explode
When resistance held in unmasks you bare,
You'll be left more to love and less feeding fear

Through The Cracks

My internal challenges were continually suppressed, increasing my anxiety, fear and self-doubt as I jumped into my teens and discovered new coping mechanisms: cigarettes, alcohol, pot, LSD, and, of course, more boys.

With no voice expression apparent, I looked for ways to justify my existence and be at peace. It was a long time coming. I enjoyed sport and having a go at anything new. Unfortunately, High School was not the nurturing place my stifled soul was looking for.

First up, auditions for art class. It was only going to be a small class, so not everyone would get in. There were a lot of us there. Precious souls, each looking for their place of acceptance and belonging. That magical place they had dreamed of, where they would be recognised as someone powerful, with something unique and beautiful to share with the world. Well, not on this teacher's watch. The system was not designed with this kind of human touch in mind. It was rigid and ruley, with no time to muck around (play). We were sat at small tables of 4-5 and were asked to draw a flower. The teacher went around the tables pointing at our sketches, saying 'yes' or 'no'. I got a 'no'. When I asked why, The teacher said that you already had to be able to draw, to be in this class. **Say what?**

How could I suck at drawing a flower?

Next up, guitar, yay 😊 This should be fun! We were instructed to grab a guitar. I grabbed one and snuggled the base of it under my left arm. The teacher told me to turn it around. It felt awkward, and I couldn't get it right. Apparently, I needed a left-handed guitar. This wasn't available, so I was sent out of this class too, not the right fit again after less than five minutes of distracted attention. There was nobody to go to, nobody to fight for your sense of belonging somewhere that brought you joy. Perhaps we could wonder who our kids would become without systemic intervention... hmmm!

Wake... up...kid...you got the dreamers disease! – New Radicals

Flashback. When I was ten, I wanted to join jazz dancing with the girl next door who was my age. I was told no, that I would probably just quit like I did with everything else. It hit me hard, and now that I had a couple more no's, my fear of starting anything I was unsure about committing to or being successful at began to lock in. The only thing I recall quitting was Girl Guides. I loved the activities, but I did not feel comfortable in the uniform, especially the beret. I was not cool with how it sat on my head, nor how my hair and ears stuck out. It didn't look right to this fussy little Virgo child, **lol**. I would not have been able to express this challenge to an adult, for fear of being told not to be silly or ridiculous, and to be reminded of it, again and again, just for fun. This common reaction and behaviour, I notice, is still something that children have to put up with, when they try to convey their discomforts to adults.

Leave me alone...won't you leave me alone...please leave me alone...now leave me alone - Helen Reddy

There was also the joke about doing flying roundhouse kicks instead of dainty jazz kicks. Although not directly pointed at me, I took it on personally too, horrified at the thought of looking rough and awkward instead of elegant and graceful.

Simple things that don't add up to much on their own, but all together make a statement, 'Sorry kid, no room at this Inn for you'. Maybe that really means that there is no room for you to be you here.

Just an Earthbound misfit... Aye! - Pink Floyd

My self-sabotaging assault weapons were building up fast. My inner child was becoming more furious and determined to fight for my best life. Not to mention that I was on the short-side list when I left school, so did not meet that requirement of joining the Police Force. I applied again several years later, passing every test except the run time and vertical jump by mere tinches. I take this as a blessing. My soul was driving my impact on humanity where it was better suited, and teaching me a thing or two differently along the way. **Hallelujah!**

I became a force to be reckoned with. The energy in my body seemed to move flat out and was difficult to control. I struggled to slow it down, function effectively and rest easy. The energy of dark consciousness was speedy. I needed to recover and re-form my slower, gentler, intuitive consciousness for peace and sanity, **aaarrrrgh!** I ate fast, spoke fast, slumped over my food, slurping and slopping with personal unawareness. My body was not comfortable, and neither was I in it. My knees and hips ached if I sat too long in one position. I felt like an old woman before my time, but I would not let anything beat me about without a fight.

And fight I did, just about anything and everything that challenged me. I offended, I defended. It wasn't pretty. I did not like being put on the spot and found ways to avoid looking at any of my bad habits. I had a deep sense of not being good or enough for or to the outside world. So I made a pact of determination to be better than that for my own benefit and good. I felt weakened by my misgivings and shortcomings and vowed at a young age to be the strongest person in the world, haha.

Soooper Dooooper! (squeely stretched out voice, please!)

It was to be many years before I could loosen and lighten up in all senses of these words. I took things personally and seriously for years. My face was stern and staunchly protected my deep-in-thought perpetual state. Please don't take it personally if I ever look at you funny or snap at you. I still have a habit of being in constant contemplation with my clairvoyance and clairaudience. Perhaps this is your reality too.

I did not see beauty or power in my human form and experience. Yet, I mustered up the energy of desire to be the strongest person in the world. It was a personal challenge that I took on literally, lol. I loved to wrestle, arm wrestle, and do anything that showed my physical strength as if it was the one thing that would get me out of my inner mess. **How cute!** *(but only when I was little)*.

I have grown to love that little girl as she redirected all the strength she had to being strong hearted instead. This little girl had another side. She felt helpless for humanity. She would dream that her dad built a small room under her bedroom and lined it with comfy beds, where the little girl would welcome others, men, women and children of all ages, with pain and sadness.

The little girl would tuck them into bed and bring around a trolley of refreshments and a soft toy. She would hold their hands and look deep into their eyes and dissolve their pains. There were no pills or potions, just loving attention. This was a regular daydream as the little girl desperately wanted everyone to feel happy and well so that she, too, would not have to experience any more pain herself. This doesn't sound too unlike what the little girl grew up to do. Yay! Maybe you can recognise this little one in your own journey.

Don't dreeeam... its... over......hey now, hey now – Crowded house

After years of not liking me very much, my parents now love the woman and parent I have become. With different views of the world than them still, they have accepted my quirkiness and the digressive dreamer in my creative, human soul, I think......**Mum? Dad?**

I'm not sure how others perceived me when I was growing up. I don't know if my behaviour was noticed enough to be considered odd or annoying. A blessing in disguise, perhaps, as I may have ended up with a few sticky labels, making it harder to peel off the layers and reveal the causes of my realities.

Yikes, no thanks!

Soul Message

What you see is not always what you get. There is no one absolute form of reality that sits well within each individual. Make your experience your own and allow others to do the same, including the children. Tamper with your tunnel vision even if you find yourself there by force. Temper it, track it for truth and tame your tedious tendencies. This is where your greatest rewards await you patiently. What is right in front of you is a gift worth opening everytime. Good, bad, right or wrong, accept the gift of your own presence.

Stare deeply into everything that steers you unwillingly and drives you on purpose. When you have come to terms of acceptance with this whole being of yours, your struggles will fizzle out. You will iron out the wrinkles that invade the twinkle in your soul's eyes. Interference from states of unawareness will step back and allow your most solid form to retrain you from your centre of core energy.

Conventional means will no longer exist in your range of probability as your being takes charge of your human experience, healing and prosperity. As you manage the to-ing and fro-ing of your personal energy, you may find greater forms of connective realities. Honour these similarities and differences that show up in other human beings too. Respect the line of time they uniquely inhabit and hold the space for them to come to all of their senses when they are ready. Beauty and power will be radiated, reflected and reciprocated.

Mmmmm, Cowabunga! - TM Ninja Turtles

4 – Give Your Heart Wings

Your journey in life could be so much more
If you give your heart wings and allow it to soar
Enjoy the ride, receive and give love
Tune in to consciousness, don't push and shove

Your whole self is ready, it sits and it waits
To pour into your body, through your soul star gate
Let go of all outcomes, opinions and facts
Allow intuition to keep you on track

Get out of the head game that once kept you trapped
Follow the path that your heart and soul mapped
No time like the present, rise up and grow
Live life like you dream it, one magical show!

Rebel With A Cause

I was a rebellious teenager, too much so for my own good. I drank myself silly, went where I wanted and came home late, if at all. I ignored curfews and did not confide in my parents one bit. I barely trusted myself, let alone anyone else. I did not appreciate or respect my parents' ways, and they did not like mine. I spent most of my time dreaming of building my own unique home or at least moving out of theirs, which I did just before I turned 18. I was working full and part-time jobs, so I didn't have time to think about anyone else but myself for a while. I had no idea of my heartlessness or hurts.

She can't remember a time... when she had felt needed – Savage Garden

Facing the anger of how you were seen, raised, disciplined and less-than-adored by your parents brings many moments of truth from all three sides of the story, yours, theirs and the combined truth. I am grateful for my eventual change in perception as I explored various courses, modalities and techniques. I moved away from the need to be a victim or feel bad, wrong or right about anything. When I made the decision to love what I loved about everyone in my life and leave the rest alone, I made peace with our past together, and my relationship with my parents grew more accepting and kind. From there, it got easier for us to appreciate each other and feel the love in our family again.

Sometimes, space is needed to cool off and re-view all aspects of your wellness and being. That's what I had to do, once I arrived in Australia and judgement was best left outside the door. I wanted deeper connections, starting with myself, and they required win-win choices to resolve disharmony. Sadly, we seem to struggle with superior or inferior egos that keep us all small and separated from the greatness in our hearts. I love my NZ family. Unfortunately, I can't be at home with them right now. We all need each other. Love you guys xxx

Soul Message

Time alone cannot heal. What you do in that time is what mends your heart.

Have you ever felt that your whole body is barely sitting on the edge? On the edge of your nerves, your dreams, your next step?. On the edge of your circumstances, of consciousness itself, other dimensions of yourself that you are yet to explore? On the edge of your abilities and capabilities? On the edge of your limitedness and your limitlessness? On the edge of a powerful calling that will allow energy to flow to you and through you for your greater good? If only you could let go, let go of your anger, your frustrations, your confusions, your sadness, your fears and worries, your burdens, your painful and exhausting commitments and responsibilities, your freeze, fright and flight modes, for just a moment long enough to surrender to it all. Surrender to all the pressure that is building up inside you, to deliver, to conform, to oblige, to show up, for anything other than yourself, for a moment, one moment, this tiny moment, could you do it?

Could you give yourself this silent and important treatment? Permission to let go, to let your sense of self go, into a state of surrender, a state of being that tells the universal energy around you that is suspending you, that you are ready to play with it. Will you allow it to come through you, to guide you to the most beautiful, powerful parts of your self, that you have never considered possible? Will you let it in? The chemical reaction of life, of love, sparking, igniting your core energy centre, and activating a sudden leap toward inner-standing of the human journey. A journey of feeling, sensing, and just being, overlooking judgment and oh so much busy-ness. Will you be here, for yourself, right now, in real-time, being real with your self for you?

Can you feel the powerful force within you that calls your name? Does it whisper, does it scream, does it yearn, does it pine for your attention? Does it scare you, a little, or a lot? Does it feel like too much for the parts of you that think you are not enough? Are you willing to give in to change? Call it in, give it a hand, give it a voice, give it the space, for it is a part of you.

The part of you that you constantly leave behind, at home, at work, at play and at large. Where are you running to? Why are you running from yourself? **You are wanted in this world.**

You are needed in this world and out in the field. You are wanted in the field of human potential. This is an energy filled with love teaching you to care more, to contribute uniquely and collectively, giving and receiving simultaneously within this field, our universal playing field. So play. Be not afraid of your greatness. Be you. Feel the deliciousness of you and all that you are, warming you, tingling and tickling your insides. Perhaps invisible and yet both recognised and felt deeply and magically. This is you. Allow tears of joy to gently caress you and your weary human body. Soothing your strict and wary mind and sailing your soul into sure and sacred personal freedom. Surrender. Breathe deep and feel this new energy come into circulation.

Allow this new energy time to integrate, to blend, and blend in within you, within your current life circumstances. Call on this new energy to provide answers before questions arise, without question, intuitively keeping you calm, collected and ever increasingly conscious, aware of the beauty of yourself, the power within yourself, and the new-found love for this little bit of magic that you have tapped into, to share with others. The magic of you is rising, to be experienced and expressed. The universe recognises you as a friend of humanity, the animal kingdom, the elements and the planet, your purpose full stop. The process and magnificence of your individual purpose will gently unfold. Be patient with yourself, with others, with all you entwine.

Sounds fabulous darling! Patsy – Absolutely Fabuous

5 – G.O.D

God's not a man who lives in the sky
That you get to meet when your life has passed by
G.O.D is a name we give something great
That lies deep within us, it's destiny innate
No one is watching and waiting for us
Just live with a purpose, in truth, without fuss

G.O.D is your spirit that drives you to find
The way to your dreams, beyond human mind
Look for its presence in all living things
Notice the love and harmony it brings
If you follow your heart, desires and passion
You will understand G.O.D and accomplish your mission

G.O.D doesn't judge you on ritual or faith
Beliefs or values or whether you pray
G.O.D doesn't punish or make your heart ache
When you give up hope or make a mistake
G.O.D is pure energy, in you and in me
Trust it will guide you, where peace sets you free

The energy of G.O.D is collective, you see
We're all part of the quantum, my friend, you and me
The pearly gates are not in the sky
They surround your kind heart as it opens and cries
Your heaven surrounds you, just open your eyes
Our enchanting world is intuitive and wise

Use it's resources to learn and to grow
Allowing your G.O.D - force energy to flow
G.O.D is the spirit in everything living
It's essence is nurtured by receiving and giving

OMG!

When I was a teenager and even into my thirties, my physiology and energy changed every time someone mentioned God or Church. I instantly felt angry and vulnerable. I didn't believe that there could possibly be a man that lived in the sky watching my every move and making decisions about my life and future based on how 'good' I was. It became so overwhelming, if I thought about it long enough, because I knew there was something much bigger to know about our existence. Yet, nothing I had heard or experienced had made sense of it all at this point.

I often wondered who or what was in control of my life and that of every other human being on the planet. Could something outside my comprehension possibly have my life planned out? Was it totally out of my control? I decided that if I died young, I would be very annoyed, and someone 'up there' somewhere would soon know and hear about it...and suffer for it! I was not impressed by the thought that my destiny and fate were already decided. I challenged anything and anyone that tried to convince me of this.

My experience and observations of religious people close to me at the time were that they lived in fear. They worried that if they did not abide by the rules of their own, their partner's or family's chosen religion, then in their minds, it would be certain that they would go somewhere terrible when they passed over. They would pray to something/someone outside of themselves to be saved after this life. **What about this life?**

I wanted my life to be in my own hands, thank you very much! In 2007, I began to learn about just that. Discovering the power of human energy, particularly our energy generating hands, was a fabulous start ... and relief!

My experience with the energy of **G.O.D (Genius Omnipresent Divinity)** told me that we are in control of most of our experiences. Expecting someone or something outside myself to deliver me a happy and comfortable life, or not, was handing over my personal controls, responsibility and credit for my unique journey and growth to someone else. **This did not sit well with me!**

I asked spirit to guide me and explain the difference between God and Religion. Know that I am not here to preach to anyone. My voice is only to present a point of view. You can take from it what you will and leave what you will not. Below are the words that followed. **Please don't shoot the Messenger!**

Soul message

5 – G.O.D

G.O.D, Genius, Omnipresent Divinity, is a collective energy force that every living thing is a part of and is part of every living thing.

Religion is a man-made ritual. It changes with the people, times, and the need to express and explain the means and meaning of creation. Man can indeed live and learn without religion and would do well to look outside it for guidance around human purpose. G.O.D is the driving force of the present, the energy in all living creatures and beings here now, and in the infinite possibilities available to all who choose them.

G.O.D is not a separate entity that holds your life in its hands. The value of each human life is here and now, in one's own hands, in the hands of your own G.O.D-liness. Open your spiritual eyes to the beauty of G.O.D in the living now. Embrace this blessing, religious or not. G.O.D is not religion. Loving thy neighbour is not religion. It is loving G.O.D. Loving G.O.D is loving thy neighbour. Loving thy neighbour is loving thyself, and loving thyself is loving thy neighbour and indeed loving G.O.D. You cannot have one without the other. You do not have to state that you love or know G.O.D for it to be so. Just be so, or not.

To be in sync with the energy of G.O.D is to love all that is without conditions. Where you cannot love, surrender to its existence and let it go. In this instance, acceptance will hold the energy of love for you. In uncertainty, let acceptance be your bridge to greater levels of knowing and G.O.D. Living with anger, fear, resentment, victimisation, and self-righteousness is not loving thyself, thy neighbour or indeed G.O.D. Look for the good in all you can, including thy small self, and you may see G.O.D in everything. G.O.D is the energy of life, the force of non-biased creativity and expansion that is of an infinite source.

Loving unconditionally, without judgement or blame, is living in the best possible energy of G.O.D. Reducing the conditions you place upon love is the way to practice your mastery of connecting to the power of G.O.D. You do not need religion to do this. Bless your existence and all that has created it. Being at peace with your genius, your omnipresence, and your divinity leaves no rights to wrong and no wrongs to right. Your peace puts another piece of love in its next place. G.O.D is consciously collective. You cannot run from it. G.O.D is the energy of creation itself. We are all of G.O.D, therefore, we are all G.O.D. (Genius Omnipresent Divinity).

Oh my giddiness, that's a lot of G.O.Ds!

6 – Intuitive

Feeling my energy, communicating with spirits
Learning to deal with their ongoing visits
Ears pricked up and fine-tuned in
To invisible creatures, causing a din

What's going on? Who's in our home?
They're all around us. We're not here alone
It's only the baby and I who're aware
I'm feeling discomfort, sadness and fear

I feel shivers and tingles through my head, toes and fingers
As spirits move around me, their eeriness lingers
What's all this about, this living nightmare?
They're walking right by me and touching my hair

For the first time, I'm terrified in my own home
Where a portal has opened for lost souls to roam
I must get this sorted for my own sanity
I feel a new journey is beginning for me

Communicating with spirit

My situation heated up in September 2005, just after my second child was born. It was a harrowing couple of years ahead of the words shared in this book. My son was barely a week old when I walked into the nursery to check on him while he was sleeping. Suddenly, I found myself experiencing what I can only describe as walking into another dimension. I could see the energy of shock waves filling the entire room as it spun with me in it. My whole body fell instantly and violently ill. I became nauseous and felt as if I would blackout and leave my body. My stomach churned as if I had food poisoning. I feared for my baby and toddler should I become unconscious or worse. My intuition guided me out of this room quickly, and I managed to call my husband at the time and mother-in-law for help. It went against the grain of my being to be vulnerable and require care from others. I felt weak and helpless. When my mother-in-law arrived to take care of the little ones, I went and laid down in the baby's room while he too slept. I felt the need to be in that room to protect him. I also did not want to wake him to move him. The room felt different again, and I managed to settle on the spare bed. Two hours or so later, I woke to the smell of three distinct fragrances, all uniquely connected to my love for my maternal grandmother. The first scent was the smell of her button tin. A magical collection of brightly coloured sparkly embellishments that I regularly tipped out onto a tray and played with as a child. It was not a smell I could describe by any other means. I questioned its arrival in my path at that moment in time as it wafted past my nose. I tested the air with a few inhalations just to be sure. As soon as I was certain of its origin, I received two more brief and distinct aromas I could only relate to my late Nana. The granny mints she kept in her knitting bag. She shared them generously with me, but I also helped myself to them as their addictive sweetness constantly called me. The third fragrance was a perfume my family used to buy for her. I was stunned at the synchronicities I was suddenly becoming conscious of. Just a few days before, I had picked up the vision of my deceased grandfather, again on my mothers side, along with the smell of tobacco ash. I asked my mum if her dad had smoked, and she said no. Sometime later, my aunt confirmed that their dad had, in fact, smoked a pipe. I had no idea how my extra senses recognised tobacco and ash rather than just smelling smoke or cigarettes.

The last time I had recalled picking up on invisible people and activities was when I was a child. That was not a time or place I wanted to return to. It felt like history was about to repeat itself, and I didn't feel ready for it. That day had me in and out of feeling normal and then suddenly sensing the energy shift as if I was being preyed upon by invisible creatures creeping up on me. It made no sense. One minute, I was happily going about my day, and the next, I felt like I needed to run or protect myself from something about to attack me. I made a few phone calls, desperately trying to find someone who may be able to help me. I was directed to a lady from the local spiritualist church. The earliest she could make it was 11am the following day. My mum and sister came to my side to defend me from any impending evil, but I was determined to get through the night without adding drama or dragging anyone else into the unknown.

I called upon all the energetic support I could remember from when I was a child, laying helpless and fearful in bed each night and the memories came flooding in. As a child, I would ask for mercy for myself and my family. I would imagine a force field of light and electricity around myself first and then each member of my family as I begged for them to be left alone, to be safe and comfortable as they slept and during waking hours. I did this for everyone in our house and a few other family members whom I felt close to. It was a nighttime vigil not to be missed, and I did it for years. I couldn't let my guard down, or someone might be taken, sadly and violently, never to be seen again. I did not welcome the return of these fears and experiences. I opposed it with every ounce of my being. I did not like the feeling of being watched and not knowing what was going on, something I had put up with too long already.

On top of the multi-dimensional portal opening in the baby's room, my childhood visitors had returned for another round of experience, greater awareness and my personal human transformation. Only this time, my eldest child was also having unusual encounters. She would avoid going to sleep and would be extremely upset and unsettled without me by her side at night. Sadly, her dad did not believe there was anything going on to worry about. So the nights I spent comforting our daughter until she slept peacefully did not go down well. It was at this time that I started to sense even more clairvoyantly, people I knew and did not know that had passed over, and random spirit needing T.L.C. When I closed my eyes at night, I would also see one eye staring at me, and then moving defensively away from me as I looked at it fair square. It hid behind other objects in my transparent visions: in clouds, under the Earth, behind windows, foliage and people. It did not feel good or right. It felt devious, secretive and spy-like. I was suspicious of this eye by day and especially at night, wondering what my intuition was showing me that I needed to take note of. It seemed to follow me everywhere, and I was always on guard. I felt like a warrior, a soldier on century duty, wary of an invisible enemy strategically positioned to take me out should I be in the wrong place at the wrong time.

The symbol of this eye that sees all became more apparent to me in the unfoldings of 2020 as humanity got a good dose of the lack of privacy reality, through multi-dimensional interference and awakening. It can be difficult to grasp the beauty and power of intuition and insightful information enough to honour and respect it. Its detail humbly expands our awareness when we allow all of our senses to interact within our body in unity. One of our great human downfalls is non-acceptance. We don't accept ourselves. We deny our experiences as real, relative or helpful. We rarely truly accept others 'out of the ordinary' experiences either. We become sceptical of the light of awareness that shines to show us the truth on our human way.

Soul Message

It is acknowleged that on one level, this was indeed an intense time of uncertainty and discomfort for the you, in human mind and form, and to the same degree, a huge time of soul-aligned revelation. You may call this your initiation into all things mystical and spiritual.... We can express it as a return trip to dimensions of self that you had not tapped into on purpose for some time. Your experiences have been in response to the amnesia you had forced upon yourself early in this particular incarnation.

Your challenges with the overwhelm of conflicting energies through the soul portal were unable to be supported sufficiently at this time, a unique journey that your Jumper Soul has taken on, in many a life line. It is true that repetition has been a thorn in your side, and you are now feeling the pain of being stuck in a loop of unawareness and unoriginality for so long, thinking that you don't know what to do in these circumstances. You have been given the opportunity to expand your awareness into the many realities that consume your energy and require your attention for self-management and to enhance your ability to be of greater service. You are now being energetically redirected to the source of your existence to feed back information and in turn, relay information and quality frequency back into the collective human experience. In due time you will recognise others on a similar journey, and the power of your collaborations will project endless light-heartedness on humanity.

Wakey, wakey, rise, and shine!

7 – Ego

I am your ego, your partner in crime
I'll push you ahead, leaving others behind
I'm with you for life. I'll thrive on your fear
Acknowledge and accept me, if you dare!

Challenge and mould me, I'll work hard for you
Let go and succeed, with wisdom in lieu
I'm just like a shadow, I'll always be near
You can let me cause havoc or teach me to care

Unlock and release me, I'll not let you down
I'll do what it takes to keep you around
Let's face it, I need you, and you need me
Together shift boundaries, expand and be free
Integrate our energies, realise our worth
As we travel together, whilst here on this Earth

Identity Crisis

The poems in this book came to me in early 2008, and the writings soon followed. So why has it taken this long to put this book together?

Sitting still has been a huge challenge for me. Even when I am not moving, my insides feel like a pack of fireworks, not only designed to make me skyrocket, burst and fall to the ground, but also with the electrical charge to uplift, surprise, and bring joy. All of this energy has felt easier to run from than to express. I did not feel worthy of rest and relaxation either. I felt my undeserving sense of self trying to justify my existence by doing things, many things, anything I could, to push away the trapped energy and emotion trying to escape my need for a suitable identity.

I have struggled to sit still forever. Focusing my attention on anything for long periods was not a happening thing. The only exception was when the writing came swiftly through my channel. It held me very strongly, and the messages were clear and easy to write. I did not have time to think. It was as if something invisible drew all my energy back to my core and directed it into its messages. Most of the time, I had no idea of what I was writing until the moment it hit the page. On re-reading it all several times, I was flabbergasted and curious about its origin. When I first decided to truth-test this idea of my intuitive writing, I called on a Medium I knew to check in with his guide for confirmation.

ChrisTian Ra's guide, Muram, told me it was coming from me. I was surprised and let out a big sigh of disappointment. 'Great!' I said. 'Who is going to listen to what I have to say? Even if they do, who will believe or understand any of this stuff?' 'It's so out there, and I don't even know if it makes sense. I will just get laughed at for being a ridiculous, uneducated dreamer!' I was nervous, scared and embarrassed at those thoughts.

It took many tools and techniques to be okay with what I was told that day. I heard that my soul had a strong connection to the human experience, not just my own, in this lifetime, but many lifetimes and to that of the whole of humanity. What?? When I settled this idea into my body, I knew it to be true, thanks to my experiences in other realms, but I did not want to believe that it was an actual thing!

My comfort along this journey came slowly as I recognised the many others who too have a strong connection to the human experience. What a relief! I was not a special unicorn burdened with high responsibilities and expectations, **phew!**.

The hardest part has been for the sensitive, un-stillable, Virgo, perfectionist in me to manage my energy and control my attention-deficit, polar-extremes and self-sabotaging thoughts long enough to organise these writings into an interesting and helpful tool. I could not easily accept that my own beauty and power were forming in the energy of these writings. I didn't easily accept that this is what I came here to share and grow with.

Today, I feel blessed with the presence of these writings. I have allowed my connection to their source, my source, to stop me from pivoting on the spot with so much anxiety. Instead, I arrived at my centre long enough to format my book strategy, mostly with a little help. Finally. Yippee!

You see, I have become accustomed to sensing and feeling so much that it is often overwhelming. I can feel all the energy of every possible failure and success of anything and everything, right in this moment, and it is exhausting. I wouldn't be surprised if you feel this way too.

I wanted a simple life, beautiful and powerful, but I did not want to stand out and be noticed. I struggled with getting too much attention for things people loved about me and ideas they thought were too crazy to entertain. **Ha ha, my parents will love that one** ☺

Don't be blinded by my light. I have a dark side too. You will feel the shadiness of it should you put me up higher than I can handle. So, no pedestal, please. I will jump off it as quick as look at you! It is not sturdy enough up there, ok? At college, I walked out of classrooms, mostly Economics, just because the teacher insisted on targeting me to answer questions. Even if I knew the answer for sure, I couldn't handle being put on the spot. I cussed at the teacher on my way out. **Sorry, Mrs Ross!**

On my first day at Intermediate I pushed my desk over and stormed out of the classroom for the same reason. Thank goodness Mrs Baker was so lovely and supportive, only I couldn't even explain why I felt so helpless, aggressive and unable to manage the energy that controlled my insides.

Some'thing bout you...makes... me feel like a dangerous woman – Ariana Grande

I did not like being looked up to or down upon. I could not find an easy resolve between the two. That said, I used to strive to be a Jill of all trades for my own empowerment and did not wish my outcomes to be judged by others. I celebrated self-mastery on my own and redefined success as the letting go of yet another insecurity or security. I did not arrive at this epiphany until my early twenties, and it took many attempts to make this philosophy work smoothly for me. It became clear to me from experience that nothing is secure or guaranteed, so rising above the need for security and adapting to shaky grounds became my quest, making peace with everything that I was not at peace with. **Fun and games!**

My recent Mantra has become – **Peace out or peace off!** – Natasha Dionne

Letting go of my reliance on anything that could be lost at a moment's notice was also recognised as the releasing of an insecurity. I saw myself as a plain and simple human being, driven by a determined and powerful soul.

I have felt like a hermit for several years now since my marriage to my children's father ended in 2013. I have discovered that I am a human being with a spirit that prefers to exist in the spaciousness of stillness, silence and the presence of my own soul over much of anything else. That is when I'm not running madly into my next new idea or craze....and hugging everyone I meet, **haha**!

This is where 'the work' begins and continues for me. I am a huge lover of exploring, expanding into and exposing the comprehensive energetic realities that consume our energy outside of what our eyes and mind alone perceive. I do love connecting with people, too, on all levels, in deep and meaningful ways, and that is where we best make use of our learnings. Mingling within the community is where we can discover all parts of our selves. It's where we practice mastering our own energy, behaviours, being, and further interconnect our life experience with others xxx

Soul Message

Let us first bust the myth that the ego must go down for one's state of well being to go up. Imagine if you will, that the ego and soul must raise each other together. There is no other way. The ego serves to protect us and drive us ahead. Even though somewhat a little hasty in its drive, the ego is a valuable life partner. ***Til life after death, do you part!***

Without the ego reminding you of your importance and magnifying your intelligence in each moment, there would be little self-care. You would be unable to lead your own way to new heights, lengths and achievements. Plodding along in a puddle of unspiritual muddle is not all the ego is good for, nor does it serve us to flush it out. It may just need a little cleanup or tweak in the right direction. An ego that is aware is an ego able to care.

Your ego will help you push through your perceived barriers and allow you to explore further human-soul potential. Your ego will permit you to share your treasures with the world and inspire others to do the same. **Hoorah!**

Can you imagine the Universe filled with joyous, dream-creating men, women and children? Your ego will support you to challenge and rebel societies standard systems and processes, the ones that stifle the soul out of a real life, and keep you from thriving and succeeding, whatever that may mean to you. When the collective energy of the typical ego grid supports human nature with compassion, love and kindness, the ability to thrive expands to more souls, and together, you ascend your vibration in creative fashion. When the ego is on everyone's side, truth and fairness prevail, and everyone wins.

Some people have mastered the practical side of human life. However, there is another whole world that does not prioritise being practical or convenient and is not concerned with finance or being economical. This side of the human existence is not hard-wired into logical states of being. It is on a spiritual and energetically diagnosed path of truth that higher levels of consciousness will expand individual and collective prosperity. And so, this is where humans must play, in the fields of morals and ethics, reverence and respect, love and integrity, as they create their chosen way to their soul's desires and destiny. This field raises the spirit in all and radiates high vibrational solutions, resolutions and outcomes for everyone. This is the road to collective merriment.

Practical means to resolve only work if the needs of the spirit/s involved are also taken care of. Humanity is finding this out, thick and fast right now. Many have yet to learn this philosophy and then be vigilant in putting it into practice for permanent restructuring of the human race track. **Geesh!**

It is a common desire to feel beautiful and powerful. Your personal lack of feeling beautiful and powerful begins to dismantle as you actively participate in the quest to know and love yourself better and not in comparison or competition with anyone else. Now there's a challenge! From there, you can practice loving others from the depths of duty and care that each deserve, even beyond their own efforts, just as you do.

It may be more of a challenge to love and care for your self in the same way. Some may find it easier to love themselves than others. Either way, there is work to be done in the domain of self-consciousness. Superior and inferior ideas and ideals imbedded in the ego-centred human psyche must be dislodged and reconnected to new pathways. The soul calls upon you to witness your will and your ways. Integrate the necessity of valuing one and all without the illusion of hierarchy and pedestals.

These strategies steal and stash energy like embezzled goods. They taint the aura of the thief and adorn them with thorny sides, pricking up the airs of the environment, keeping them stuck in fiction and out of flow. **Holy moly!**

Well, thank you, my little poetic soul ☺

8 – Guiding Light

Following my guiding light
Unconscious by day, conscious by night
Where am I going, where will it lead?
It's full of surprises, lessons to heed
Embrace and endure all experience the same
Share from the source of where you once came

The good, the bad, the ugly you store
Laugh through the tears, the points you find sore
You're bigger than this. They're not who you are
Find your own footing, raise your own bar
Life is a precious and magical game
Treat it as such, like your innermost flame

The one that's inside you and drives you to tread
Where the ground is both new, and you're likely to dread
Chase your fears down, face them, don't hide
So the energy surrounding them can only subside
Feel free of the baggage that no longer serves you
Breathe deep and relax without limits or curfew

Live life to the full, have fun, be a rebel
Step outside the square and to the next level
Step down and step deep to find the real you
Without judgement or blame, you will find what is true

The truth is the best and most potent of all
To where love, compassion and consciousness call
The Universe needs you, there's no time to rest
Accelerate evolution, experience your best!

Dream Weaver

It took years and effort to move past the sufferings of my own experiences with spirit and energy and perceptions of my existence and behaviours. I felt like I was consciously addressing my biggest fears in my dream state, where I found myself reliving my insecurities and worse case scenarios with others, changing my responses, creating more harmonious outcomes and ultimately, new versions of my awakening self. It's like I had created an extension of myself to deal with things behind the original scenes. This extension helped me release some of the energy of unworthiness and weakness from my vulnerable body while bypassing my unaware, life-sucking human mind.

My dreams were showing me the polarities of everything that existed, just to confuse me, I'm sure. I had virtual experiences, recognising perceptions of good vs evil, as above, so below, better or worse etc., and the pros and cons of every single scenario. And yet, my daytime experiences made me feel like I was functioning from a not so conscious autopilot, driving me from places I did not want to live by. I wanted to dismantle this repetitive programming and embody the energy of eternity that was playing in my field. I felt it work for and against me as I hibernated in my own bubble of deep and dark light expression and beingness. **What a headful!**

I began to give the clear intent just before bed that a particular challenge would be resolved overnight. I would allow myself to relax my body and let whatever would be, be. Others teach this as zero-point energy. This worked well. The process became easier as I began to clear and resolve misaligned interactions, relationships and possibilities in NOW time. It became a daily activity to breathe deep through my unawareness and chaos as my soul revealed its hidden abilities and delved into the life-less agendas of my human self. Breathing deep and asking the right questions of my self helped me redesign my daily experiences by authentic means and let false formulating go. **Slowly but surely, my light reached a tipping point. Thank goodness!**

Soul Message

Your inner flame is the energy of your desires. For many, these desires sit too long on the back burner. You hope and wish for your inspiration to arise in this flame to magically carry you to your divine destiny. You despise having to navigate the process of elimination that bears your right of passage to conscious evolution. Some of you are uncertain for many years, about exactly what it is that lights your fire, let alone how to spread it. You don't give yourself the time, space and patience to discover and explore what you love about your own unique existence and being. You are mainly distracted by doing what you are taught and told, and you try to squeeze into existing programs and systems.

Love is just a mushy word you avoid to evade the perception of weakness. So you miss the power of vulnerability and the point of your present life on Earth. You are mostly trained to follow those before you and end up sinking in unwell, trodden grounds. Some of you are lucky enough to fall into jobs or interests you enjoy or have a natural talent for, sooner rather than later. Sadly, some of you will never know what sparks your personal joy or believe that you are worthy of it on a regular basis. Others may never arrive there at all. Think about what amazes you. Who are you in awe of? Follow every tiny thread of inspiration and excitement within you. They are calling you to play with your loving soul. There is always time to ignite your own divine spark if you provide the right frequency matches to that which you wish to experience.

Twinkle Twinkle...You little star!

The way to move forward and change lives from a sad and self-sacrificial existence is to uncover the subconscious replays and less conscious behaviours driven by them. The ones that leave you unfulfilled, no matter how hard you try. The aim is to identify your hidden pains and insecurities and release the emotional charge they hold in your mind and physical body.

To begin, you must choose to practice the sound of silence so that you may hear the roar of your private hurts and misunderstandings, loud and clear. From silence, you can listen with all of your senses to the more conscious whispers of your internal messenger too. This voice that lies within you holds deeper meaning for, and of, your unique self, to be, do and have beauty and power beyond five sensory realities and responsibilities. Be with this deep, meaningful messenger. It is you, authentically so. This voice is the will of your unique soul. It is only invisible if you do not see it and get to know it intimately. It is your purpose to recognise this voice, serve your self with what it communicates to you and utilise it to serve others. Share from the voice of your soul, make it available to all for the healing of humanity.

Subconscious patterns may lay deep and yet be expressed superficially in reversed psychological ways. They hold the energy that gets under your skin, pushes your buttons and pulls your legs out from under you in an attempt to get your undivided attention, love and release. Instead, the unconscious traveller may pay more attention to their fights in fanciful ways and drama, not usually of the most nurturing kind. And so, this little game of pass the buck becomes entangled in a much larger matrix of chaos and uncertainty. When you act from a state other than love and reverence for all that is, you shirk responsibility for your own behaviour, deflecting judgments and blame for personal challenges and irritations. You begin to see others as the ignorant ones, unkind and unjust.

Like a child you deem naughty, as they learn the dos and don'ts of your fear-fueled world, so too are the adults learning to challenge and conquer the maze of predictive text that has ruled unnecessarily and for eons. It's not just what you are doing that tires you. It is who, and how you are being that exhausts you and wears your body out. It is the self-less love and spiritual neglect that lets you and gets you down. Keeping your soul in secret denies you a great life style, leaving you pain-filled, weary and struggling to get out of survival mode.

Why? And for what?

From the moment you attempt to follow your own instincts in your family environment, you are given direction, for better or for worse. You explore with your curious minds the sensual delights you experience through your able body, observing and interacting with people and things in your surroundings. As you learn to talk, walk, choose, discover and absorb, you are redirected to the needs or expectations of others. You are instructed to smile for Mummy, walk to Daddy, don't touch that, play with this, put this on, be nice, give me a hug, say thank you and so on. You are plastered with kisses from anyone and everyone and expected to receive them with gratitude, readily and willingly. When you share your feelings truthfully, you are told not to be rude. If you find yourselves retaliating when you feel you have been treated unfairly, it is demanded that you be good and gentle otherwise the opposite would come your way tenfold. If you find yourself not feeling confident or happy, you are teased, told to pick up your lip or suck it up. You are relied upon to care for younger siblings without question as if you too should be emotionally and physically capable and equally responsible.

As you grow, you are sent outside to amuse yourself until it is convenient to be called in, even if what you longed to do was inside. You are expected to serve your parents' needs for an ear or shoulder to unleash volatile emotions created by the overuse of control in their own upbringing and personal relationships. No one is immune to all of this behaviour. Some master a tinch of it here and there. So the journey becomes to unravel the soul's core energy, as the power of the psyche's wind up and are put in their best place.

9 – Let Go

Let go of your baggage, shed many tears
Wash away your worries and fears
Peel off a tired old layer of skin
And into a new skin, prepare to jump in

Step forward, step up, be clear, don't bluff
See and accept you've no use for "guff"
When you do, you will feel a new energy build
Reinvent yourself consciously, experienced and skilled

When you've cut your ties to chaos and strife
You'll be high on the love of your fabulous life
For lessons you've learned and wisdom you've gained
As you welcome in pleasure and heal your pain.

Freedom of choice, in all things to do
Is available "NOW", release it in you
Support you, my friend, is all I can do
For helping yourself is how you'll get through

Excess baggage

Quote – 'Leave the drama for the stage and the fighting for the mat' – Natasha Dionne

Some of us seem to fit in quite happily to the systems provided by society, while some of us don't. We do our best to find our way and work with information and opportunities that are readily shared and available. For some of us, there is another will and way calling us. It can be a challenging time, one that requires self-discipline and understanding of the highest order. It requires permission from ourselves to go places alone, to look deep into all that we are, and explore everything that controls us robotically.

At this time, I was becoming aware of my sensitivity to energy and spirit. I felt my desperate need to relax and meditate. I had to learn how, first. It was not natural for me to sit still and allow the energies that consumed me to be there as equals. I preferred to dash from their madness. Making sense of the frequencies and dimensions I was unknowingly tapping into was becoming a must.

I attended evening mediation classes, which encouraged me to be gentle on myself as I opened up to new possibilities. I did not even know what that meant. It was the start of an extremely emotional year for me. I'm sure I spent most of 2007 sobbing tears that could have been released much earlier in smaller bursts had

I not expected myself to be so tough, pretending that nothing I felt within me mattered.

I was literally weighed down with stuff that existed in my emotional body and laid heavy on my heart. I was in desperate need of a change in routine and direction. As I searched through a spiritual magazine for something to catch my eye, I came across a Louise Hay Leadership Workshop in Perth. It turned out to be about 10 minutes drive from some close family members. I immediately ran the possibility of an all-in-one trip past my husband, to which he agreed.

I had no idea that my emotional state was about to get a whole lot worse before it got better. Growing up in Boganville (not actually), I felt like I had to be hardened to survive. Crying was not an option. It was considered soft and weak. Being gentle was (please excuse the offensive lingo as I get my point across) for poofters and pansies. These derogatory terms were used to break the spirit, sort the girls from the boys and show who's boss. Inappropriate names that two beautiful young men in our own family would once have become labelled with and victims of. Not cool! We even labelled one of our brothers as one just because he liked to wear his pants high-waisted and tuck his t-shirts in. Regrettably, we called him Trisha. Sorry, little brother. ☹

If you weren't seen to be rough and tough, you were girly as if this was a bad thing. If you stood out for being too big, too small, too anything different, you were slapped with a sarcastic label, as if it were funny. Every action was reacted to in disharmonious ways. Perhaps a reflection of perpetuating generational grief, dished out willy nilly, without caution or care. The inferior ego can cause terrible damage on its quest to raise its opinion of itself. I swore and cursed as a teenager and fought back, and well, sometimes I still do. Only now it's with more of a humorous undertone and not directed at anyone, except usually my own doubts and disgrace, lol.

By the time I hit my mid-twenties, I was waking up to my own troubling behaviours and vowed to ditch all acts of unkindness. I decided that no matter what anyone said or did to me, I was not going to stoop low enough to react or retaliate in a hurtful manner. I was going to rise above my anger, sadness and insecurities. I would fight this thing in me, this cycle that harboured never-ending guilt, judgement, blame, shame and invisible pain. I was going to let it all die out, by returning myself to purity and innocence, two newborn elements I treasured and missed. I was going to enter this energy with all my love and might, to snap myself out of the old and into the new. Whenever I felt a blow, mentally, emotionally or spiritually, I would let it hit me and observe my feelings flying off the handle or sinking my heart and smile. I would let them do their thing on my insides and watch them spin out as they eventually wound themselves down. I did not offer them the chance to spray gunk onto another party. I came to love this newfound response ability. I felt continuously empowered to manage my own energy better. Bigger efforts brought better times. Self-mastery became my mission, and it had a ripple effect on my relationships with family. **Happy days!**

In the past, I had instinctively used visualisation techniques to lessen the issues I had around certain events in my life. This prepared me somewhat for this turbulent time. The emotion that flooded my being was gut-wrenching. I was afraid of letting go of all I had ever known, thought I knew and did not know. Even my dreams had upped the ante with visions of violent deaths. I gave the intent that they purely symbolised the end of my current way of life, not my actual life.

As I prepared for my wonderful trip to new beginnings, I sensed that a healing journey had already been triggered. For some reason, my eyes seemed to be calling me in from our large bathroom mirror. Each time I looked into it, I recognised myself less than before. All I could see was an ugly creature behind a serious face with a scary demeanour. My inner grief was reflecting my pains and worries, raising them to the surface and refusing to hide them from my awareness any longer. As I looked in my eyes with persistence, all I could see was a monster. ***I looked like a monster!*** Hard, mean, angry, irritated and sad. I couldn't find anything to like about myself.

My head kept reminding me that I had experienced many supercharged moments when I loved being me. I was mindful of how blessed and abundant I was, but it wasn't enough to stop me from feeling miserable. I did not understand. I thought I was good at reasoning with my troubles and forging ahead with my next venture. However, I was unaware that by not allowing myself to feel any pain, I was harbouring it, hoarding it in my body like trash, expecting it to decompose itself. This haphazardness had greatly affected my quality of life. There was no room for pretending here now.

The self-sabotaging masked woman had to move out!

The following two months saw me say goodbye to some old stories that had patched me together. I sauntered reluctantly in a daze towards a softer, more vulnerable and self-responsive version of myself. A me that would learn how to increase the flow of feminine energy in and around myself and feel at home with it. Using the Louise Hay YCHYL Workbook exercises to guide me through my feelings and find the origins left me exhausted. Facing these memories, experiences and relationships within family dynamics was not an easy job, especially when I felt like I was more of a pain than a pleasure to anyone.

I felt like my heart was so stretched and bogged down with the energy of every trauma and grievance that had ever entered my life, big or small, everything undealt with honestly, openly, truthfully, and fairly resolved.

Perhaps even the energy of experience from previous incarnations, generations and humanity in general occupied space in my tiny, dense form. I seemed to feel everything going around! It was clearly time to meet that baggage, face to face, and return some to sender. With divine intervention, I began to sort through what was mine and clear the lot out. **Blimey, what a task!**

I had filed many hurts in the too-hard basket to deal with later. But later never came until now. As I worked through the **LHYCHYL Workbook**, everything that wanted out came out. It's important to note that it doesn't matter what comes out, or who thinks that your experience was like that or not at all, that it wasn't that bad or that you shouldn't feel this way. You do feel this way, and that is that. Not wanting to recognize your feelings as true or justified just continues the suffering and keeps you functioning less than humanly effective. I found it easier to go through this process away from my family so as not to offend or hurt anyone. My worries were not their problem. I acknowledged and accepted every feeling I had. I granted each one access to pass through me. This made for better odds of releasing the pain around my memories for good.

Emotional baggage was hidden and stored in my body. It was obvious. My face was red, my hair was wirey, and my body appeared swollen. Every part of me was working hard because I was miserable. My mind and soul suffered too. It was a packaged deal.

I managed to tuck my grief under a layer or push it into a corner of my body somewhere, while I soldiered on being positive. A decision I made longer ago than I can remember. Whilst this served me well and got me through to my late 30's, it was time to lighten the load. My physical, emotional and mental wellbeing depended on it. Not to mention my beautiful family, who did not deserve the ripple effect of my controlling, impulsive energy, taking its toll.

I did not realise at the time that my soul required my complete attention. I needed to follow her voice to learn about who I came here to be and lean into her creative enlightenments. It was time to take the reins of my future, and of course, it had to start at the beginning, clearing out unwanted memories and feelings of spaces in time that no longer exist, maybe never existed as I imagined them. For years, I had no idea that I was giving my energy to many things that trapped me in a cycle of low-vibe life. Intellectually and emotionally, I was still stuck on other people's ideas, opinions or expectations. I could not think for myself and therefore had no idea what I thought or felt about anything, important or otherwise. I seemed to have put my own desires, intentions and philosophies on hold, not realizing their purpose or importance.

Writing this first poem was a huge challenge for me and an even bigger accomplishment. I was unsure what I was writing about until it entered my head out of the blue around 5am one morning. It was when I looked at what I had written that I decided it was a poem. I was so in awe of it that I read it over and over. I gave the intent that I receive more of this valuable information, and I promised to write and take heed of it. Although the words flowed to me easily over a few weeks without any effort on my part, it could have been a very different story.

For years, I had thoughts, words, and ideas come into my head, but I would not take the time to write them down. I doubted I could have something so intriguing to share and did not want to be a 'know-all, know-nothing', another popular childhood remark. Now, I am very grateful for all my inspiration. I enjoy transforming it into something useful as it hits my energy field. I still need help organising it all, though... **Aaaargh**!

That year was the hardest. I was still learning the ropes as a Mum to two small children and facing many issues surrounding unhealthy lifestyle patterns. I was on a relentless journey into the unknown depths of self-discovery. My health was suffering on all levels, body, soul and mind.

During this time, logic was nowhere to be seen. This invisible force took charge, leaving me feeling completely out of control and uncertain about life in general and my wacky, unpredictable future.

9 – Let Go

It was time to take a good look at my perceptions, habits and behavioural patterns, so that I could make a conscious decision about what I did and did not want to give my energy to. ***Positive changes were not going to find me on their own!***

I began to acknowledge every issue and situation in my life that had left me feeling hurt, insignificant, angry and confused. I accepted that my perceptions and experiences were mine alone. I was willing to be wrong and change the habits and reactions that had kept me unhappy. I did what I could to interrupt the flow of detrimental thoughts. I let myself feel the emotions that plagued me to do so. I even allowed the emptiness to sit and stay without trying to filler, it up. Mastering these attributes has brought me a great deal of peace.

Once I progressed past my insecurities, worries and fears, I found a love for life that took me to deeper levels of authentic being. Variety returned to me in new, creative ways, including writing and, most recently, drawing. I now have the energy to explore them as and when I please, without holding back.

If you have no emotional baggage then there is less energy required to carry yourself around. You feel lighter. It's like replacing old clothes that no longer fit you with more comfortable ones. You feel more relaxed and confident within yourself. There is less pushing from your spirit to deal with unresolved issues as you are already aware and have begun the process of letting go. Daring to be different encourages spiritual growth and creativity. Being afraid to do what feels natural to you is a waste of energy and life. The layers of consciousness are deep. Judging or blaming yourself takes you nowhere fast. Self-criticism will only deepen the wounds of your past and make them harder to heal. Just acknowledge, accept and allow it to be. Know that you made the best decision you could with the information you had at the time and commit to never making the same mistake. **I can now love being me!** We are all in this world together, to live, love and share. How great would the world be if we all reflected only the best of ourselves upon each other in every moment.

Oh, what a... strange... magic! E.L.O

Soul Message

Are you ready to be an anchor of light? Use this light of yours to diffuse the sparks of any injustice that may fly at you and the flames that fuel darkness in all forms, ideas and concepts. Leave no soul behind. Instead, everyone beside each other in a non-linear fashion. It is not possible to truly see someone that you place righteously behind you. To see them fully, allow their very being to exist beside you, as you walk your own ways. Observe, ask questions of the needs of their spirit, the fears of their minds and the loves of their hearts. Tread gently, soul-fully, respectfully and kindly to resolve your challenges with others. This is how you begin to play full out in your integrity. It is integral to your soul's potential and unfolding. Anchor your light of commitment on the grounds of collective human-spiritual contentment.

It's like in the movies when the good guy has the bad guy cornered or trapped in a compromising position, where he could easily take his life and put an end to his own suffering from this source of pain. You sit on the edge of your seat, yelling at the screen, 'do it! Do it! Waste him! Finish him off! Don't let him go, he'll be back for you!' **Don't be such a nice guy! This is ridiculous! Aaaargh! But!**

The good guy so predictably pauses, puts a stop to his violent outrage, calms his inner farm, looks the villain in the eyes, showing all his might, warning him that this is his very last chance (again) and then lets him go. A certain amount of respect is recognised as the technically defeated gangster walks, flies or jumps away, continuing the saga of good vs evil.

A bit like our inner battles of drama and fighting, we can become masters of our own resistance. The power lies in our choice, whether we hold tight and stick to our guns or we surrender and let go of our neediness to be right or win at all costs. The power for change lives on when the baddie does not get destroyed. He has been saved for another day and mission, with hope from the good side, that he evaluates his tainted ways and transfer to the light, for life. It is hoped that you won't be drawn in again, to become another victim, with no other option now, but to play for the other team from the depths of your own low vibrational frequencies.

Every time we surrender our offensiveness, we instantly become more energetically protected and our ability to experience a beautiful, powerful existence increases. The more we let go of our need to fight or control from a sense of superiority or survival, the less we find ourselves called to defend ourselves in sticky situations. Let this be your mantra. With ease and grace, I am free to be me. Allow your core energy to radiate and enrapture everyone it touches. **Let everything else go xxx**

10 – The World Is Your Oyster

The world is your oyster, don't be deceived
You can share in prosperity, no need for greed
There are plenty of pearls in the depths of emotion
To find them, you need only love and devotion
Of love you're created, part Heaven and Earth
You've endured through lifetimes, dimensions and birth

The tunnel may be narrow, the road may be long
Whatever you do, always right, never wrong
Knowing what's best for 'you' is essential
To support and nurture your fullest potential
With food for the soul and a strong yearning heart
Follow your wishes, they want you to start

Create your best life in this world and beyond
Back to the source of all light to re-bond
No beginning, no end, competition or race
It's all about you, so steady your pace
Be kind to yourself, for it's all an illusion
Forgive and forget past hurts and confusion

Tomorrow you'll find new direction to play
To live and to learn from a special new way
Much stronger you'll get, both inside and out
Your passion, your purpose, your being will sprout

From your centre below to your centre above
Your energy electric with the purest of love
For the world and for others, yourself, all the same
Value connection more than fortune and fame

Pain and gain

Moving from New Zealand to Australia in January 2008 was a natural move for me. I am still happy with this decision, considering the circumstance around my being a single parent. Sadly, it was tinged with discomfort, as a few of those closest to me thought I was running away, thinking that I thought I was better than them in some way. 🙁

It may have appeared that way, but I wasn't finding my place where I was. I couldn't explain it or the unusual, mostly spiritual, happenings. I had to hold myself together and take time out of the usual to head into the unknown. I was excited, but it was a delicate time for everyone. We had sold all our property and could not secure anything new in NZ. Every time we tried to purchase a home or a piece of land, something would get in the way, and the deal would fall through. I knew there was a stronger force at play, and it seemed like something within me was driving it.

For years, I felt Australia calling me, and at this time, I pondered the idea of making that move now. My husband agreed although it seems, he did not feel at home here like I did. I loved the adventure of something new. I wasn't worried about work or money. **One of my weaknesses, gulp!** We had enough at that time, I thought. I just needed a space to work out my experiences and what to do with them all. I felt like I was going to go crackers if I didn't. The Gold

Coast provided the support I needed for my spiritual journey to continue. I am pleased that I followed my calling, even though it felt like I was dawdling through a psychedelic zone.

Not every soul takes on this idea of spiritual journeying. Mine did, and it was pushing and pulling me in all directions, opening me up to all sorts of unconventional experiences. My husband was not impressed, and so the path to separation began without me knowing. My family was extremely sad when we left. My mum ran after me as I headed towards the boarding gate. She sobbed at the reality of not seeing and touching us in person for a while. Our little ones were almost five and two and a half. I was not prepared for her pain in those moments. Sorry Mum xxx

My soul was calling me elsewhere, and Australia was not that far away in my book. Our connection was a little vulnerable as I had said I wanted nobody at the airport to say goodbye. My mum accepted my wish until the last moment. Tough, I know, but I did not want to feel bad or wrong about going. I needed to go, but I didn't understand why, then. I had not seen my mum cry like that before, not even when we lost my youngest brother on the roads in 1999. I think the expectation on herself to stay strong was engraved in her heart when her own dad passed away when she was just 13. He had suffered a blood clot to the brain and left his precious body on the kitchen floor, leaving behind two little girls and a disabled wife. I wish I could help my mum heal those pains. Talking about things sometimes makes it feel worse before it gets easier. I honour my mum's strength and know that she enjoys hands-on healing. I love working with her when we are together, and I give the intent that I get to travel and be with her again soon.

Following those pearls are about opening up to greater amounts of love and understanding. Communication and being real with myself and others is where I personally find my treasures. I think I am getting better at it. **Hot diggidy!**

I now call both Australia and New Zealand home, but I am mostly solar-powered, so for me, NZ is best for visits. *I love my sunshine!*

Soul Message

The energy of possibility floats around in our collective realities, filled with every human want and need. It waits for individual and collaborative, magnetic attraction and generous distribution, without fear of failure, rejection, losing someone or something, jealousy, being second bested or whatever runs through the narrow mind. Our planet and fellow men and women have all the supporting resources needed to offer prosperity to everyone who wants it and to those unable to reach for it themselves. There is little excuse for having so many souls with desperate basic unfulfilled needs. This me vs. y'all mentality plays a big role in the substandard human psyche we are entrained with. Personal power becomes more potent than competition and control when we work together in unison. One humanity, beautiful cause, powerful effect.

When we feel like we are competing against others, it is a sign that we have not yet tuned into our unique soul frequency. The lack of flow into an individual's life directly relates to personal unawareness, conditional kindness, limited confidence and lack of action. A sense of self-unworthiness leads us to outsource the possibility of our dreams and desires coming true, along with our responses and capabilities. We give the intent that another's unique talents, presence, and abilities alone will get 'us' over our line of poverty because our human soul balancing act has not yet been mastered. It is often to our children that we disrespectfully pass on that which we disown. Our mission must be to restore in self, faith and freedom to fly. From here, we can be personally fulfilled and of service to others to achieve the same.

Let go of ill-intended words or actions directed at you by others as soon as you can. Refocus your attention on your own respectful responses, thoughts, feelings and behaviours. Nurture the full expression of your existence and allow others to do the same, unhindered by your own insecurities.

10 – The World Is Your Oyster

Your human experience will be a continuous cycle of learning through many beginnings and endings. Sometimes, something new will begin that allows the old to come to a smooth and natural end. Other things must come to an end before the space is available and open to receiving. Then something new can enter your field with its possibility. It will depend on what you fill your daily life with and all it encompasses. What you give your energy to and that which you allow to drain it, including the fear that worries your mind, the sadness that sinks your heart, the burdens you carry on your shoulders and the resistance in your gut. This all fogs out the energy of your soul and further weighs down your dense human form. It depends on the signs you choose to follow and if you try so hard to think everything through, rather than let go of thought and allow your instincts to guide you genuinely in your interactions without bias or condemnation.

The greatness in you is much like that of a pearl in an oyster. You will only discover it upon cracking open the shell that protects it. The greatness in you does not rely on expectations or ideals. Competition, selfishness and greed are old energy ways of moving yourself forward, up ladders or into prime spots for prosperity. They come from a place of self-satisfaction, and give and take transacting, instead of giving and receiving from a place of authentic energy, love and fulfilment. There are many pearls of wisdom and creativity deep inside each of us. A journey to the core of your own being will raise them to the surface for everyone to enjoy. There are no shortcuts to self-exploration. You will find many wonderful destinations if you allow the process of self-activation to begin.

Sit still enough to listen to your heart and give free rein to your imagination. Do not concern yourself with where others are in their evolution. They, too, will have much to learn and offer. They may have similar lessons and interests from different mediums. Forgive yourself and others for past issues. Accept them for what they are so that you can move forward without the weight of the past. There will be no benefit to continuing the pain in your mind, as this has a flow-on effect that drains the spirit and damages the undeserving body.

When you accept events of the past and the uncertainty of the future, the present moment entertains you with a sense of renewable energy and wonderment. Your self-esteem will strengthen, empowering the real and beauty-filled you to emerge with purpose and grace.

Learn to be kind to yourself as naturally as you are to others. Being nurtured and loved by your self is a requirement for more pleasurable life experiences and healthy, sustainable relationships with others. The quality of your relationships reflect the state of your self-love reservoirs. when you raise the standard of attention and focus you give yourself, you are gifted with awareness, From this awareness, you will be shown the elements inside you that have felt unloved, unlovable and less likely to succeed in your endeavours because of it.

Your neighbours will live on their own frequency. They, too, will be struggling with their sense of self, even if it is not visible to you. Everyone deserves the same respect, dignity and humility. The higher the amounts of these attributes that your energy projects towards them, the easier it is for everyone to reflect greatness upon each other. From there, we can venture on with more pearls than poison leading our way.

Love what you love about people and leave the rest alone. Don't go there. Create your boundaries and keep your distance. Do not give your time and energy to any unnecessary fighting or drama.

Your issues with others may be driven by false insecurities, unfairly unleashed upon the opposition in unfathomable ways. Do not accept everything as your own or their own problem. Track your own record and steer clear of theirs. Let them work themselves out and move forward in your own unique presence and grace. This dismantles pent-up tension and dissonant energy. It stops the ripples of pain travelling to the next person and so on. Flow-on effects that hold victims to their stories, drains spirits, and damages inflamed human matter. Others too may follow their own greatness if there is less toxicity to play with. There is no room for mind games in the heart space. However, there is plenty of room in the heart to help the mind mature and expand the bearer into more refined states of being. Self-esteem strengthens as we come back to clear out and refill our own space. The free and beautiful you is now ready to re-emerge.

Don't blame it on the sunshine (or your ex). ***Don't blame it on the ....la la la!*** Jackson 5

11 – Flying High

Full of life and flying high
Throughout the Cosmos and beautiful skies
Giving intent for manifestation
One with the Universe and co-creation

Unravelling... my conscious mind
Checking for mastery...hoping to find
Emotions on edge, energy low
Desperately wanting back into my flow

Once I have found it, no letting go
Loving the warmth of my essence, my glow
Accepting my outer shell, knowing what's inside
Is far more connected to my spiritual lifetime ride

I am present. I'm here in the "NOW"
No need to worry about where, why or how
All will be revealed to me in divine right time
No expectations, no pressure of a life sublime

Beauty accepts the Beast

I felt like I was going for it. The sky bared no limit. I was working with my intuitive healing techniques on clients and in their homes. I was helping women heal from unfruitful pregnancies, communicating with earthbound spirits and moving them on willingly. I was healing energy in spaces so kiddies could sleep better, and families could understand why they were restless in the first place. I was helping people resolve minor health issues, loving the energy of insights and connection, and giving and receiving with what was coming to me and through me. I was grateful for every experience to be proactive in this mysterious field and re-energising what matters most.

I found that the more I worked with energy, the more alive I felt and the more useful I became to myself and others. It was a magical feeling and time, but no time to think that it would stay that way forever. There was always a new client, relationship or family challenge to address, as the energies of others reached out for help from my field of expertise. These energies touched and tackled me many moments, day and night. I had to create boundaries around when I was willing and unwilling to be available. Bedtime was out of bounds. However, I was still occasionally frightened awake by random trouble makers and peace seekers, experienced clairvoyantly and clairsentiently. As I woke each morning, I would observe the energy I was sensing.

It was regularly intense, so I would question if it was mine. This was a process of awareness, tracking and calibration as I worked out, or not, where this energy was coming from, what it was trying to tell me and what I could do about it. Sometimes a knot would be felt in my gut, or a nervous feeling would stick with me and then later in the day, I would discover its origin was someone I knew, going through a tough time. It would eventually be revealed and released as I communicated with this person in person, or with the energy remotely, supporting their energetic needs and comfort. Healing with animals was also a highlight at this time. I searched my thoughts, feelings and actions daily for signs of inspiration, evolution and spiritual-human mastery.

This seemed increasingly important to me. I felt I needed proof of getting somewhere and had to justify my being here. I double-checked everything relating to myself and took responsibility for all of my thoughts, emotions and actions. I noticed I no longer felt irritated or anxious about some things that had previously bothered me. This confirmed to me that I had put some matters to rest. **Yeeha!** Little did I know that what goes up must come down. It was not long before I realised that this heightened state of awareness would make me work to maintain it.

I began to let go of my physical appearance being a top priority. Its importance seemed to fade out of my awareness as I felt a different strain of beauty and power take precedence within me. My perception of appearing less than was not a match for my feelings of being more than that. I sensed expansion as my body tried hard to accommodate the energy of purity and soul contained within it without burning out. I learned that how things appear are not a one-stop reality. From this experience, I became determined to wear my beauty on the inside. **Because I'm a lady, that's why!** Marie - Aristocats

I suddenly felt like I was headed towards a different world, again. I didn't know how that would look or what I would encounter next. The road to'd and fro'd for sure. However, I was getting in the groove of letting go and not having to be in a particular place at a certain time. **Yassss!**

Soul Message

The journey of the human soul is rarely direct. It is in this indirectness that you will gain your experience and work your way through the maze of human consciousness to the playing field of the superconscious. Make peace with your human-ness, for it does not know what it does not know, haha. Allow yourself time and space to process and follow your greatness, even if others are challenged by it. You will be in a better position to understand and support their needs once you have taken care of your own, on the levels that many do not dare go.

A spiritual quest need not seem so woo-woo. It is more of a mission to take care of the spiritual needs of humanity. That is, raising the spirit's needs to be seen, expressed and loved for what they have incarnated with. This is a role for the aligned healer. Woo-woo is merely a 'whoa! I can't go there, it's incomprehensible to me, I don't understand it, it makes me feel weak and vulnerable, and I have no desire to soften up to that mush'. That mush is a must for heart-centred being, be it in relationships, business or otherwise. New energy and multi-paradigm realities become available to those who get out of the head game and into the heart match of the spirit in disguise.

You are not entrained with this, so the struggle of the human soul existence takes on the need for courage to go beyond the just-getting-by experience.

Well, that was short and sweet! Just like me, haha ☺

12 – Depression

Depression is dark, depression is deep
Not a condition so healthy to keep
Destiny's child knows what to do
She's all around us, for within us she grew

From seeds we've all planted, day after day
Waiting so patiently for her turn to say
Where the truth for her lies, so deep in her heart
Where love and compassion try hard not to part

With support, she'll remember before she forgets
Live life to the full, no limits nor regrets
She'll look forward, not back, with trust and acceptance
Without shame or guilt and little resistance

She'll break down her barriers with strength in her stride
She'll have a great impact on those at her side
For her lessons have led her to where she now stands
With her own many experiences of life and death first hand

12 – Depression

The Jug cord

The pang of the jug cord on my behind was a friendly reminder to get in line, do what I was told and not cause trouble for my parents. You know the drill! The trouble mostly being not doing the chores I was told to do, and refusing to adhere to commands that expected more of me than I was willing to give. I had enough going on in my less visible world to deal with and did not like my time and energy being directed to joyless exercises. It irritated me big time and depressed my tiny big spirit! The jug cord was the weapon of the '70s, designed to make you behave a certain way and jump into gear at a moment's notice, a bit like being in the Army. I was so terrified of being hit that I would beg one of my little brothers to take the blame. I believed he was more loved and therefore, less likely to get hit. Kids! Sorry, Damo. ☹

I vowed never to raise a hand to my own children. They did, however, receive one good wallop each from me, sending a double banger pang of pain right to my heart. My eldest copped it for playing hide and seek one too many times in the aisles of the $2 shop, which pushed me over the line with my suppressed anger and fear of losing her. She was two. The other child took his hit when his sister complained that he had repeatedly poked her in the face with a pencil. It only took me seconds to fly down to his room and read his body language. The look of defiance and guilt was all over him. He was two and a half. She was five. It was a behaviour that triggered my righteous need to nip the energy of violence in the bud, with, interestingly enough... a dose of my own trigger-happy aggression. I find it both sad and hilarious how we think as human beings that unleashing ourselves upon our kiddies is somehow helpful and a necessary evil sometimes. I'm pleased to say that my kids don't remember these dark moments, but I feel better being open about the places I have come from. It would be all too easy to pretend that it was no big deal to me, or for them, but that is not the way of the conscious warrior in the true hero's journey.

I have accepted the parts of me that felt out of control in those moments, and I accept responsibility for the actions I took. I let go of the guilt I once had that tarnished my perfect parenting ideal. I also admire the change of ways my dad had on matters of discipline over the years, as he left the jug cord where it belonged and chose a more heartfelt approach to understanding human and childhood behaviours. Considering the grief and violence he experienced in his own childhood, I feel sadder about his journey than mine. As a two year old, he watched his father stab his mother from behind the couch. He was separated from his three older brothers and put into foster care, when his dad went to prison. His mum left the country and fled for her life, never to be seen in the flesh again. My life was no comparison.

12 – Depression

In 2007, I was blessed to be visited by my paternal grandfather in spirit, begging for forgiveness and allowing me to support the release of his grief-stricken emotional energy and the lack of connection with his boys. I am always grateful for these opportunities to transform energy and relieve spirit of their burdens and baggage.

As I write this experience of diluting violence throughout the generations, my beautiful dad is being held in care at Te Omanga Hospice. He is on that much morphine to kill the pain that the essence of his being is sedated. I give the intent that his spirit chooses to gain strength in this loving place and stay with us a little longer. I long to see him full of beans again, feeling the love and joy he worked hard for and earned. I wish he knew he had the ability to remove the pain and stored trauma of a tormenting childhood in the way that I have been blessed to know and experience. I feel like both of our souls have incarnated on some level to heal a small part of humanity with our experiences, our voices and our hearts in our own subtle ways. Recognizing the violation in all fighting and drama, all anger and hatred, all abuse, all judgement and blame, all self-sabotage and harm and all avoidance, putting a stop to the madness in our lineage as much as two lone souls possibly can. I love you Dad xxx

Soul Message

Every effort made to intercept shadows of self and disrupt violent streaks makes a difference to the next generation and heals the backline of previous generations. Sadly, many find themselves in too deep to see that they too have become part of the problem, not recognizing the ways they violate their own sacredness and steal energy off others simultaneously. They do not realize that they are separating themselves from the very things they most desire (love, connection and joy) by lashing out at others in their imaginary pecking orders.

The energy of depression and anxiety ceases to exist within you when the energy of expectation is not imposed and control lives only on the inside of your personal boundaries. The first step towards your own love and joy comes when you decide to love what you love about others and leave the rest alone. Come back to your own beings, doings and makings. Permit yourself enough space from anything and anyone that violates it, in any way, big or small.

Allow others to do the same without your input. Their shoes are not yours to walk in, nor their behaviours yours to fix. They too may be struggling to follow a trail of love and joy . You will understand the simplicity of this message when you have a handle on your own full expression. Perspectives and desires are in the hands of the beholder. This includes allowing your children more freedom and choice to play with creative possibilities in their human experience, just as your family before you fought for, in their own internal or external ways, for various reasons.

Allow yourself to expand the expression of your deep resting soul and create a safe space for your nearest and dearest to follow the vibe. Children will respond more readily than adults as they are not stuck in so many old ways. The sooner you start addressing what sustains and saps your energy for life itself, the more impressed you will find yourself with what you have to offer.

Practicality, convenience, can't be bothered-ness, because I said-ness, righteousness, superiority/hierarchy, financial hardships and unemotional entrainment can stand in the way of everyone's greatness. Even without dependents to cater for, many adults still have challenges around the black and white box that houses their mind's most unreasonable certainties.

I know we've come a long way

We're changing day to day

But tell me... where do the children play? – Cat Stevens

13 – Kundalini

Feeling uneasy, there's nowhere to hide
Searching for strength and courage inside
Kundalini is rising, I feel it vibrate
It's time for my work to begin in this State

I love what I do, I do what I love
I wish to be peaceful and free as a dove
New beginnings await me, but endings come first
What is it inside me that wants me to burst?

It's happening soon, no mercy, no excuse
It just wants out, it has nothing to lose
The demons I'll face will be worth it, I know
It will finally allow me to breathe and grow
My future awaits me, my soul as my guide
I'll reach out to grab it, hands no longer tied

13 – Kundalini

Shaking Foundations

This experience happened to me when I was trying to get pregnant for the first time and held resistance to every element of that reality at the same time, including putting on weight, feeling something moving inside me, giving up work and not contributing financially. The possibility of being unwell and having to care for someone else anyway. All those things scared me and woke me at night. It held me in fright and rattled my nervous system regularly. I felt inadequate, vulnerable and less than my friends and family, who were becoming parents at the drop of a hat. I felt the energy of annoyance and the desire to lash out whenever anyone asked me when I was going to give my husband a child, **GRRRRR!** It felt like they had one over me, and **I was not appy Jan!**

I decided to pretend that it did not bother me and came up with a couple of responses to any nosey queries about my infertility. I would say, 'what do you mean? We already have three! And laugh it off, or I would talk about adopting because there were already enough unloved little ones in the world. I did deeply feel this but somehow making my own felt more romantic and accomplished.

This kundalini intervention put an end to my fear of becoming or not becoming pregnant, as if by way of magic. I did not understand it at the time. However, this experience was the welcome relief I needed to energetically hold the space of possibility within me, without inter- fear-ance. It was still a few years before I was blessed with two precious babes, however, I was better prepared now, for either outcome.

Some say a sudden spiritual awakening usually occurs when someone has been involved in a traumatic event. When I heard this in the past, I wondered if the person saying it thought this was more of an imaginary experience brought on by mental and emotional health issues that require mainstream interventions. I guess in a sense, it is the energy of our thoughts, feelings, words and actions that trigger extreme opposite electrical charges and then intuitively, the soul provides a third option to the mix that brings the receiver to a gap in the middle. The most important thing is the awakening of the personalities to the existence of the spirit that has come to play in this temple of ours. Its aim is to lead us to all senses of self and others harmoniouisly, Even if only eventually, after many trials or incarnations.

Kundalini energy can be felt like orgasmic energy, highly sensitive, intimate and sexual. This is how it was for me. This feeling came from the letting go of all inhibitions in that moment, submersing myself in total acceptance and surrender. Opening myself up to receive, on all levels, from all dimensions of delightfulness. Allowing my humble physical body to be filled with the power of pure light and the unbeatable feeling of pure love. As its fire raged through me, spontaneous kundalini energy melted away my triggers to anything but the joy of being alive. It momentarily overrode vulnerability, uncertainty and indecision, to just be with my-self, alone and in company, in all of my unglorified glory. I felt all of this movement in my body for less than a minute. **It was amazing!**

Further on, I noticed kundalini energy rising just before another change in my set routines. I could feel the shifts of awareness between all that is dark and light, daily. These shifts are like signposts, indicators that a new way of thinking, feeling and experiencing is on the way. There is no escaping the electrical charge that comes through me at these times. It won't allow me to budge until the new course is set in my awareness. It only happens every year or two as clients come and go and my location sends me packing again. I feel the pressure of polarity constantly battling around me in the atmosphere, removing the cogs in my anatomy as I gain a new perspective of my own and the collective human experience.

My energy centres once spun like wheels of fortune, though they feel more connected than separate these days, if I notice them at all. When these powerful spirals of energy were initiated in my body, I gave the intent that I would be heading towards the possibility of a new and improved destiny. I hoped that others I was connected to would also become aware of their existence from a whole new space and perspective.

This is not an energy that everyone is keen to play with. I personally did not make any effort to invoke it. I do not believe it is an energy separate from me to be afraid of. It's a powerful energy that activates change, be it occasional or constant. If you are afraid of change on one level and excited about it on another level, and you struggle to make decisions, you may well feel the energy of your own kundalini rising up to support you with the letting go and moving forward process. That has been my experience of it.

Soul Message

The Kundalini is an energy of pure and knowing consciousness. Present at the birth of every human baby. Kundalini energy is secured within the base of the newborn's spine. This energy is the powerhouse of human-soul transformation and is gently released throughout the human experience, where intuition, ease and grace are witnessed, encouraged and taught, above all else.

Daily and incidental drama and fighting for the right to be right, seen and heard, leads to a life of little learning and growing beyond insecurities and pain. The battle between the truth of the individual soul on its path to enlightenment and the entrained egoic personality protectors can cause the human to suffer immensely, prolonging self-pity, self-doubt, self-neglect and self-sabotage.

In these numbing states, the transformational Kundalini energy is denied, refused, rejected and trapped by the sceptical and cynical minds of the less aware. This action forces the kundalini energy down, away and into a corner where fighting for your real-life eventually becomes paramount to your divine survival.

So, a game of tug o' war begins between the energy of the soul that wants one to know thyself, vs. the energy of the personalities in all their disorder. That is, they are not in order of alignment with the soul's purpose, intent and plans for a unique and fulfilling human experience. They get in the way with their fears, and it becomes like an arm wrestle, where the pressure between sides is held against each other until one side weakens and eventually surrenders its resistance. The pressure peaks and releases its hold on the human biology, physiology and anatomy. The pent-up tension flies like a rocket up through the body and out of the magnetic field until its force wanes and declines, leaving the human consciousness to return to Earth, more grounded, balanced and less concerned about their chronic inner conflicts. And now, although somewhat confused, the mind has let go of the need to control the soul's expression with egoic views of human experiences, discomfort and expectations.

Spontaneous kundalini energy release can be felt by the coming together of the dark and light within us. The strongest energies from both sides, the ring leaders, jumping in the ring to settle a cause once and for all. This coming together is not necessarily a one-time event. It can happen repeatedly in large waves or as a gentle system on slow release. It can be experienced continuously after a sudden, shocking and undeniable initial awakening. The journey is individual, depending on the demons within the psyche and the diamonds buried with the spirit inside.

The release of the kundalini energy can be like turning on a tap. The flow of water/energy can either drip slowly or flow fast. Fast-flowing kundalini energy can make it difficult for the human to comprehend, manage and handle effectively without getting drained and confused. While kundalini energy is highly cleansing of unnecessary dirt and grit, the after-effects may leave us drowning in liquid gold. It could leave us feeling overwhelmed with all the original insights, further awakenings and new beginnings flooding our fragile, physiological, emotional and first eye-opening gates.

The kundalini rising can be scary, depending on your personal beliefs and willingness to accept your sensations as a sign of necessary and involuntary change. It was not exactly scary for me, although it made me weary and suspicious at the time. **Haha!** The rising of this life force energy begins to increase circulation. The circulation of truth, circulation of lies and circulation in general, to give you a sense of new information to base your views of the world upon. This rising energy can trigger a regurgitation of old traits, patterns and traumas, giving you the opportunity to live them over or revisit the memories and deal with them more harmoniously. Thus releasing their hold on your insides and freeing you up to move forward with greater purpose.

A spontaneous kundalini experience can raise itself in an earth-quaking vibration, shattering the restraints of the human mind and technically knocking out everything in opposition to its rite of passage.

The kundalini energy can be seen at work when lessons are learned, behaviours are changed, and a state of love, understanding and acceptance is regained quickly. Where lessons are resisted, mental, emotional, physical and spiritual wellness, calm and peacefulness elude us. Then we attract much of what we fear, ignore, deny or try to run from.

Spontaneous kundalini energy surges are experienced when the inner polarities of desire and resistance are at an equally strong peak and go into battle. Kundalini is purely life force energy. It is only noticeably forced when we have an inner conflict between two opposing ideas, notions or desires and we cannot decide. We cannot find a way to accept one over the other. So, tension builds, adding stress and sometimes panic. The pros and cons of each choice are equally valued by us, so we procrastinate too hard and long as we sit on the fence.

Sometimes, it is because we are avoiding our soul's needs. So, the pressure of suppressing them builds up so much that our deepest energy of desire within the purest consciousness of who we are takes over and pushes the mind's energy of reluctance and resistance out of our own way, in self-defence.

It need not be seen as some kind of mystical experience or unexplained phenomena that only happens to a few lucky or powerful people. It may instead be quite the opposite for some.

This experience is a signpost, a symptom of a greater cause brewing than what we are living, or an energetic realignment in the offing. It may be an opportunity for you to pay attention to your greater needs for a change in consciousness. This energy is forging the way to a new and extremely different style of life than you have been exposed to, one that your Soul can no longer tolerate being separated from.

Not all spiritually awakened people will experience this kind of intense energy release as they may have surrendered to their intuitive flow and direction before the energy build-up became too strong for the Soul to bear. Through an ongoing process of self-awareness, personal development and evolution/adaption, the kundalini energy is always rising. Continuously raising your personal vibration and entraining you with greater presence and acceptance of the love and lessons in your humble human life.

What's known as the serpent energy or described as a coil of life force, prana or chi, and present in the base of your spine at birth is purely an analogy. Much like poetry, we like to show and tell a story and give it an extra touch of meaning, fullness and enlightenment to satisfy our paranormal curiosities and spiritual wonderment.

Since your original experience, it has been a continuous ride to address stagnant energy and raise the spirit within. You could say that the idea of kundalini energy symbolises the rising of the power behind your soul and its mission, the aware one embedded in the matrix, of as yet, uninformed consciousness. The increase of this intelligent energy brings relief with the integration of understanding and acceptance that now peaks and forms a state of knowing. It releases excess electrical charge around truths and mistruths. These shifts of energy and consciousness can be sensed subtly or felt intensely, both leaving you feeling different than before. Often, you are no longer bothered by some of your usual dramas and conflicts. The resistance has left the building. Life force is literally in each of your hands. Feel the magnetic push and pull of energy within you as you reach out and give someone in need some hands-on love and attention. Notice what happens when you look them in the eyes with compassion and unconditional acceptance at the same time. It is a great catalyst for surrender and melting away pain. Feel the love and magic return to their body. A great feeling for you too. Xxx

Wow, that's some serious stuff though, aye?

Phen-om-ena, doot doo doo doo doo! (Sung to the tune of Mahna Mahna) - The Muppets

14 – Winds Of Change

Winds of change are in the air
Let go and let G.O.D of the Universe steer
Give up on logic, disease of the mind
Leave all shoulds, can'ts and worries behind

Surrender a life of survival and fear
Be open to change, find your own flair
Let your soul lead you, get out of your way
Accept intuition, honour it, obey
Embrace new direction, love and let go
Tune in to your heart, welcome new flow

U.F.Orb

As parents, we tend to want something for our own children that we thought we never had. Something we wanted to experience to feel safe, loved, accepted and good enough to spend quality time with. I felt alone and unsafe at night. So, I wanted to make sure my kids went to bed feeling loved, supported, understood and relaxed. I wanted to read them books every night before bed, and I did. I wanted it to be a fun time of the highest quality experience for their sacred little beings. It was one of my favourite things to do, but it didn't stop my eldest from having similar nighttime experiences as her devoted mum. She still had visitors, invisible to the naked eye but clearly obvious to both of us that they were not just nana's and grandad's in spirit popping in to say hi. Beings of unusual frequencies from other dimensional realities, with their own uncomfortable agenda, seemed to wander in regularly, unannounced. **Who you gonna call?** (Mum!)...Ghost Busters Theme Song

And so, the saga of interdimensional living and surviving continued. I was starting to think that maybe this weird stuff would be with me for the long haul. One of our early unexplained experiences together was in my daughter's room when she was around 12 months old. We were lying on the spare bed as I breastfed her. Her fingers and nails grabbed at me as if trying to get even closer, and her feet fidgeted and wriggled constantly. I could feel the vibration of footsteps walking up the hallway to our baby's room. The door opened, and the footsteps continued towards us. I'm not joking. **(Big EEK here!)**

Every ounce of energy within me made its way to my gut and pushed my heart to start thumping outside my chest. The medicine bottles on the bedside table began to clang as if someone was fumbling around them, looking for something in the dark. I couldn't handle the suspense or the closeness of this invisible activity. So I sat up abruptly, holding my baby close to my body, desperately wanting to run from the room and scream....And then suddenly, as my legs hung over the side of the bed, my calves experienced an intense heat and burning sensation as a ball of fire/bright light/orb, goodness knows what exactly, shot out from under the bed, across the room diagonally, right in front of us and disappeared into the opposite corner of the room. **FUUUDGE CAKES!**

Everything I had in me nearly jumped out of my body and died of fright. But then, interestingly, the energy quickly dispersed and subsided as we both fell into a deep state of calm. **Bizarre!** I wondered if the source of this experience was trying to push me out of a repetitive family cycle that was not a fit for me.

Much to my disappointment, it soon became clear that we would, in fact, be on the move. I didn't understand fully yet, but I knew it had something to do with me, energy and spirit. We had to get someone in to do some healing on the house and property first. I couldn't imagine the next owners having similar nightmares.

I took my time letting go of the family home and the treasures I loved. This new adventure in the pipeline refused to align me with anything old, already done or lacking creativity.

Ohhhh..... do the hokey pokey!!

On the day we walked around our 1903 home for the last time, the spirits of all Jones family members lined the walls. They clapped and nodded in approval of our choice to move on and leave their traditional values behind. I was gutted and emotional. It was my favourite home, and I wanted to be there forever. The character of this home was magical to me, the timber, the sash windows, the lead lights and the high ceilings. I loved Petone, minus the earthquakes. I was going to miss this family home. **Bye Richmond Street xxx**

We stayed with my parents for 5-6 weeks after selling the house, as we looked for somewhere else to set up home. During this time, I got up to go to the bathroom one evening. Strangely, I felt myself leave my body and saw myself walking through the actual door. The next thing I know, I come to, and I'm in a heap at the foot of the door, on the bedroom side. I don't know what happened or how much time had elapsed, but my whole left side was tingley and numb. It was winter, and I had flu-like symptoms too. **Not fun!**

Energy started to charge through my entire body on and off. The palms of my hands throbbed with electricity. The heat was so intense that I kept them out of the blankets, free to let the energy flow out in full force until it slowed itself down. Otherwise, I felt like I was trapping the heat in my body. My feet were the same. I still found myself temporarily having to keep my extremities out of the bed covers to keep a comfortable temperature, as this feeling seemed to burn another layer of burdens off my being. In my awareness, it tore down another level of semi-consciousness. It pushed me to reorganise my thoughts, feelings and actions towards whatever I was not feeling one hundred percent about.

This still happens to me sometimes. With this energy comes a reality of truth about my current situation and its circumstances. A truth that I have not yet seen or taken into account. It lights my misunderstandings on fire, shedding another load of shame and shooting me toward higher ground. **It creates space for acceptance...or not, and new beginnings....or not!** My body senses and sees the change in full swing. It feels the unapologetic rage of flames blowing away my resistance. It is not a terrible experience, just another day in the life of my soul, destroying old ways in this being of evolution. It is like the Phoenix, rising out of its own ashes, to reform and recreate itself from a fresh offering of life-giving force.

Burning me, like fire...I like what you're doing now.... fire! – The Pointer Sisters

Soul Message

Just like the change of seasons, your Winter is rolling out, and your Spring is rolling in. It may not feel like it right now, but this change of atmosphere brings fresh energy to you with new beginnings. Open your heart and welcome a new season of life. Allow a new level of experience to invite your presence and self-acceptance, no matter where you are or where you are called. It is time for you to learn to let go of time in the current popular context. This moment in time does not exist to slow you down. You will come to use this timelessness to track and measure certain elements along your life path. This includes much of what lies in the space between what you spend your awareness on and where your dreams can take you. It is no longer useful to immerse yourself in the controls of timing to justify all that you are. You may find that it controls your ability to open up to the spaciousness required to explore your soul's creative insights, abilities and potential. Sitting in space and embodying the energy of timelessness will give your human self the power to turn off the pressure of time and work actively and diligently towards the gifts you are destined to complement humanity with. You could call this change a step towards timeless being. Feel everything else burn away with love. Keep it simple, sunshine!

Aaah, beautiful and powerful! xxx

15 – Time To Come Out

It's time to come out now and lay in my bed
To face all the monsters I have and I dread
To clear all the grief I hold deep inside
To relax my whole body, front, back and sides
I've never felt safe or secure, though I've tried
So desperate to seek, resolve and not hide

I've searched, and I've found, learnt, and I've cried
I've often felt trapped, and my soul has but died
The answers have come through in various ways
It's taken this long to work through the maze
Am I supported? I feel so unsure
It hurts me immensely and weakens my core

My being has suffered trauma of past
I feel a big shift. I hope it will last
I want to feel joy back in my heart
Pumped through my blood, a welcome fresh start
Rejuvenate my cells, ill from anger and guilt
Let them wither away, the pain I have built

With them send my worries and fears
Hidden and trapped, mistaken for years
Now I'll be left with the best I can be
The greatness, the wisdom, the love that is me
I'll share it with those who wish to enlighten
Their minds, their souls, their spirits to brighten

When will this end, and how will I know
How to transcend to where consciousness flows?
The love in my life awaits to be found
When centred above, feet firm on the ground

Facing The Shadow

At this time, our family of four was living in Gilston. We had one child at school and the other at preschool a couple of days each week. I was at home tinkering in my healing room, feeling another wave of change coming. **Batten down the hatches ....!**

Our daughter wasn't settling at night as usual, so I spent my early evenings with her until she fell into a deep sleep. I knew something was up, but I didn't know what exactly. She began to talk about things chasing her that nobody else could see, and this started to scare me. She told me about seeing me being sucked into a black hole and said I knew the guy who was pushing me into it. Great! Another spooky story that no one will believe...hmmm. Our son was sleeping ok but was also talking about similar happenings. He was only three and was asleep whenever my daughter and I talked about this stuff. **A new nightmare had begun!**

My husband (at the time) was annoyed at me for all the weirdness going on. His opinion was that I was projecting all my fears from my own childhood onto our kids. Although I felt some truth in this, I did not know what to do about it. It couldn't be just me, could it? This was not a fun time. The energy of frustration and confusion built up so strong that it seemed to follow me around the house. Everywhere I went, I sensed an angry energy. Although I didn't feel that it was mine, I knew I had to deal with it in this moment, for our family's sake. The feeling got so strong that I had to call in for help. It was over my head, and I had my angry husband telling me that it had something to do with me, and **I better sort it out, pronto!**

I had not been in Australia very long but had luckily worked at a psychic/healing expo and made a few contacts. At this event, there was a woman that made funny noises, snapped her fingers a lot and moved in ways I had never seen. I recall joking to my husband about not letting me get that weird. Sorry, Shely xxx. After making a few phone calls, I was referred to this lady. Interesting! She took my call, and I booked an appointment for two days later, although by now, **my body was trembling and shaking uncontrollably with this energy that seemed to be stalking me.**

This woman asked me questions about how I thought all this came about and how we were going to make it move out. All the while, I was filled with anger and fury like never before. So we decided to follow my desire to scream the house down. **Sorry neighbours!** I had no idea that was in me. It was the longest, loudest noise I had ever made. It released a huge amount of pressure from my body instantly. I didn't feel that it was all over yet though, so I kept my booking and went to her home for more.

Everything about me was rough, tough and hard. Even my hair was strong and unmanageable. My head was so sensitive and tightly held that I couldn't wear my hair up. It hurt!. At primary school, my Mum would sometimes put my hair in a ponytail, and I would rip it out as soon as she was out of sight. It made me feel like screaming. My body only began to loosen up in my late thirties when I started to embrace and face my soul. The more inner work I did, the more knots within me released, and the more flexible every part of me became, including my mind, opinions, beliefs and openness to change.

At age 52, I can now safely put my hair up without sensitivity or pain and going doo-lally! It has taken me that long to de-stress my head and relax when I have something on it, including sunhats. My kids love it. They get to see more of me. My face doesn't need to hide under my pains and strains anymore.

Soul Message

The traumatised human spirit is like a loaded gun. Any little bump in the road that takes your finger off the desired pulse is an incident waiting to happen. Beware of the bumps as they happen and before they come again. Step back and observe yourself. Take your finger away from the trigger. Unload your ammo and find the best way to calm your nervous system. Taking a deep breath is of the utmost importance here as you breathe freedom into those body parts that only get to see the light when you explode with unstoppable presence, inappropriately, uncontrollably and unlovingly. Find the space to give them some air time. Air your fears and worries in a safe environment. Disarm yourself, and your life-style threatening triggers will not be the same. Now you will view them as memories, energetic storage of traumas gone by, allowing your human self to remember, without trapping yourself, in a future fuelled by past pain.

Groovy baby!

16 – Transformation

A wondrous transformation awaits
As we've searched for, discovered and flooded the gates
That secured the secrets and protected the mould
A state of reality that once had a hold

A process in progress is happening now
To my soul I'm committed, I solemnly vow
I've faced many challenges with nervous unease
Now redundant are perceptions of sub-personalities

Created by me to help with resistance
Of a helpless, judgmental, unjustified existence
The result was quite different from what was expected
It led to uncertainty and feeling rejected

With balanced personalities tucked deep in my heart
I thank them all dearly, let go and restart
With fresh new ideas, no ties and no drama
I can now read purpose, lessons and Karma

It's time to integrate mind, body and soul
For now, it's my aim, responsibility and goal
Where will it take me? I really don't know
Will the road be direct or step to and fro?

Little Miss Personality Plus

My appointment day came, and although I was feeling less tense, I knew something big was happening today. So off I go to see Shely again. I got comfy on the healing table, and as she began to speak, **whoosh! My energy body fizzed and fussed around me instantly and relentlessly.** I think it was sorting through the mess of my unseen parts that wanted to be loved and let loose that day. This was my introduction to the energy of sub personality traits that I had created to cope, conquer and function when I was not comfortable in my own skin. Sadly, this was much of the time.

I had created 26 versions of myself, or persona's, to get me through each challenging time and relationship. I was avoiding the vulnerability I felt inside. This energy swirled around my middle and relieved itself from my chest mostly as Shely ran through the names of these identities that inhabited my human space. There was the victim, you know, the one that has been hard done by. There was the faultless one, the one who could do no wrong. There was the weak one, the warrior, the helpless one, the guilty one, the one that aims to please everyone, the useless one, the angry one and so on. **It seemed like there was a personality for every occasion. Huh?** All these may just sound like crazy behaviours and ideas. However, I learnt first hand that the energy of over or underactive personas can cause havoc in your experience and, of course, in your body.

Their energy literally followed me around like a shadow because they were my shadow. But I was disowning them. My kids were picking this up too, yikes! These energies wanted me to look, see and integrate their support for me, so they could no longer give my experience false positives or false negatives. This may sound a little odd. These personas took on an energy of their own, but each, only in certain circumstances. For example, I was very confident as a parent, a little submissive to my boss, a victim to my peers where I felt I needed to belong and share similar stories, and still a teacher to anyone and everyone who would listen.

All these hats we wear tell their own stories and have a unique vibe. Some we use more than others and not so consciously. These roles my energy played with became like entities of their own, waiting for me to dismantle the excess energy around them as they tried to protect me from feeling my trauma and grief. After two and a half hours on the healing table and another 90 minutes chatting to Shely, I felt lighter, freer and more sound in my understanding of my recent events. Thank goodness, **now my family could find peace forever...maybe? Pretty please!**

Soul Message

When thoughts, ideas, feelings and desires are unexpressed and kept to oneself, they create tension. They build-up fear, worry, uncertainty, confusion, frustration, anxiety, anger and resentment within you. Every under-attended need and over charged emotion grows, as a tower of pent up energy rises. Within it, mistaken identities shake your foundations and set you up to crack and crumble under the pressure of previous misunderstandings and misguided adventures.

You will feel a sense of dis-ease, unease and fuzziness. All physical systems have to work harder to bring your body fluids back into natural flow and purpose. Your state of persona affairs is emptying from the too-hard basket. **What a kerfuffle!**

The art of intuitive energy healing you experienced has increased the circulation of your thoughts, ideas, feelings and desires, bringing them to the surface, out into the open for your acknowledgement and action. Your experiences, perceptions of them and personality traits have drained your energy for too long, giving you a false sense of security and self-consciousness, leaving you in a state of confused living.

This work has encouraged stagnant energy to wake up and move. It has released excess electromagnetic energy around your unhelpful states of being for a more gentle and continuous flow. You may now feel peace a little more often, haha. When you avoid feelings, boundaries and actions of self-truth, you generate a lesser quality form of self, an imposter of restless energy if you will, which compromises your wellness on all levels. This is how much of your dis-ease comes about. And now your body begins to malfunction. You see things, hear things and sense things that this energy bombards you with. Your body and mind appear to cope under these chaotic conditions. It works against high odds to re-harmonise itself, with your soul-filled self in it.

This energy work is a re-alignment of truth within your whole being, as it addresses every energetic part of you. In action, it re-forms the connection between your head and your heart, installs a new order of how you go about your daily business and improves the condition of your physical body. Your soul's agenda stays high, mighty and strong with humble acceptance as you learn a new way to go about your life. These personas will not die or leave you forever. They are equally valued in the right places. For now, they have done their time with you. It is a tumultuous world to grasp and ground in. A plane of existence where egos collide and spirits entwine for a greater understanding of themselves and each other. ***It's an adventure!***

Wake me up ...before you go go! - Wham

17 – Clearing Pain

Clearing the mind, opening my heart
Feeling the pressure in each body part
Releasing old energy, no longer trapped
My heart and soul becoming unwrapped

Diamonds are forever, sacred templates included
Activating full presence, no longer secluded
Being enlightened by unique experience
Willing to live a more conscious existence

Galactic energy, serving a blow
Charging and zooming, high and low
Ready and steady, holding my core
Pinning me down to help me feel more

As quantum forces collude and collide
Alternative realities, I cannot hide
Loving and honouring, all attributes
Suspended in space, as my history transmutes
A new form of wisdom, cleansing the air
My strength and abilities, kicked into gear

Pain, Pain, Go Away!

I sometimes find myself releasing copious amounts of acute pain. I thank these pains for showing themselves in this time and space, for giving me the opportunity to be fully accountable for my whole reality. I wave them goodbye as they feel seen, heard and leave my body. These pains come from my unresting mental, emotional and spiritual misunderstandings. In my experience as a healer, we call upon pain to communicate with us. We hold the calmest space for it to feel safe in and rise into.

As the pain surfaces, it is released from the beholder as much as they are ready to let it go. We give the intent that the pain reaches beyond its current resistance to the freedom on the other side. We give the intent that the healee decides that they are personally worthy enough to experience this freedom, no matter the cause, or the benefits of holding it. Our pain-body consists of neglected energy around the unknown, unwanted, unloved and unaddressed. My journey with relieving pain has not included toxic tonics or medications. These tend to prolong the effects in many cases and stop you from feeling what's really going on.

As I lay in bed on this particular morning, with another round of pure light and energy raging through my veins, a new message arrived to explain what was happening to me.

Soul Message

You are not dying. You are not unwell. You came in with this trauma, and you have accumulated and absorbed even more. As you feel safer in your own experience and expression, this energy will free your body of pain. It takes time. It is a process. It is many processes of an intricate nature, deciphering many codes of perceived misconduct. It is moving through you, out of you, not into you. Stick with it, persevere. It is all you can do. Be here with it. Give it space to move and be witnessed. This is all it asks. Don't hold on to it. Don't resist its need for attention. Accept it as it soars toward your consciousness, for the love you have yet to remember it for, the love you forgot to give yourself upon its creation. Go with this flow, do the best you can in this moment. Let it pass.

Me: I feel filled with anxieties and fear at a moment's notice, and sheer excitement and euphoria, the next. It is confusing and challenging.

Soul: You are a spiritual warrior, of sorts, busting out to move closer to your self, your purest of consciousness. Sitting, thinking, feeling and speaking slowly is difficult when your energy is raging through you with high velocity. But sometimes, we must speed it all up to shift and sift, then slow it down with less attachments. You will notice the difference. Feeling at one with everything does not usually bring comfort.

You will feel the trauma and pain as well as the love and the joy in everything at once.

Me - It is too much. It is too full.

Soul - It overflows through you and around you. It leaves you spinning around the Universe, in and out of your body, trying to feel better. In this state, you will know that you truly are energy first, and form second. Your energy holds a higher quality frequency than your form. You feel like you are spinning as fast as you imagine the Earth. You feel like you are going nowhere at the speed of light. Your human journey, where you are learning to re-torque your own walk, is quite a show! Let go of the uncontrollable that you attempt to control, shift gears and grab hold of only what you can. I am not asking you to let go of the love you have for what you have lost but let go of your desperate need to change the impossible.

Your energy is bringing your body up to speed with your light and progress. You are clearing out and levelling up, realigning with new elements of evolution. New frequencies are creating space within you. Let it settle. New codes and downloads are available to you as your body upgrades.

Ce- le bra-tion time, come on! – Kool And The Gang

Me - I don't think so!

18 – Windows To The Soul

Our eyes are the windows to our soul
Through them, we see what has taken its toll
Everyone's life is just the same
Nothing more to lose, nothing less to gain
Our heart desires fulfilment, our head strives for success
Our minds create havoc, our heart's left with the mess

If you want something different, be willing to change
Be open to trying the new and the strange
Challenge your securities and insecurities too
It's a credible way to the dark depths of you
This is where you will find most significant growth
To rewrite your life contract and consider a new oath

An oath to yourself, mind, body and soul
Be responsible, empowering, regain self-control
Take charge of your journey, energy and love
Wear your heart on your sleeve 'til it fits like a glove
For a heart that's locked up and protected with doubt
Does not let love roll in or radiate out

Our heart yearns to share love, not to miss out
To give and receive love's, what life's all about
Make no excuses, no judgement or blame
Get along with goodness, let peacefulness rein

Panic Attacks

I have noticed that my eyes glow whenever I'm doing what I love: channelling, writing, healing, speaking about energy and resolving pain and suffering. I look like a different being altogether, and of course, I am. I am present with the core of my being, with my soul. I allow her to drive my daily routine, as per our biggest loves and natural abilities. I project and exude all the love she has for herself, for me, for the space and opportunity to play fully in those moments. I know when I'm in flow these days, my eyes feel like crystals, sparkly and powerful. My energy feels light. I experience a natural high, thanks to the frequency my entire being briefly holds. You may have noticed this in yourself and others too.

With the pros of doing soul-filled work also comes the cons. Sometimes we are proactive in our unique quests to explore and expand within and beyond the practical material world. Other times, we experience constriction. One of my constrictions in recent years came in the form of what I call 'Panic Attacks', although it's not what you might expect. Let me explain.

It feels like I am trapped in a box and need to burst out, only I can't burst out of fresh air. I am stuck between dark and light, or even life and death, and I just have to wait it out as if I am in transition in no woman's land. I am not in my head at this time. This is a physical sensation. It feels like I am being contained in an environment too small to inhabit and function effectively in. I use my mind to do what I can to keep my body calm and breathing. My mind knows there is no threat, nothing to fear and nothing wrong. It does not see or sense a problem. And still, my body feels disconnected from my cool, calm logic and severely restricted by my environment. **What the heck?**

I have to move a little, then still myself for a while. I get out of bed, go to the toilet, stare at the white floor tiles, then go back to my room to feel if it is ok to turn a light on. I turn on the base that my selenite crystal sits on. I adjust the shade and brightness until I feel I can cope with it. I got it! I look at my bed and go to sit down. I feel agitated. I can't do it. I need to keep moving and distracting myself from this feeling of no way out. I wonder where I can go to feel at peace.

I walk downstairs and go through similar motions. I turn on the light in our tiny kitchen. The entrance to our little townhouse, the open lounge and the stairwell remain semi-dark. I feel I can cope with the mix of dark and light from here...in this brief moment. And now I'm on the move again, thinking, feeling, breathing manually, purposefully, trying to work my way out of this invisible control. I try to let go of all thought and sensation. It doesn't help. **What to do now, at 12.15am?**

I go to the back door and peek under the blinds to the outside. I feel ok-ish. In a few seconds, I have to move again, back upstairs. Where next? I go to my room. I am tired. Can I settle and sleep now? The feeling of entrapment pulls me in. I reach for my water bottle, sipping away at the feeling of ever-deepening dehydration. It distracts me a little. Then I am off again, slapping my palms on my thighs, chanting 'get in your body Tash, be present, be here now, come back to your body Tash.' I get to the bathroom, run the tap, cup my palms and fill them with water. I splash my face, over and over, telling myself to 'wakeup Tash, wake up! It's going to be ok soon. Still, I am uneasy. **Panic stations!**

I feel like there is not enough light coming in to me. I am running out. The world is running out of light. The darkness is staying for good. No light can get in, anywhere. It's not that I am afraid of the dark or what lurks in it. I don't feel unsafe outside at night, even on my own, even in this situation. It's not that simple. It's more like an uninvited, acute sense of discomfort from both the lack of light, and the overwhelming presence of light, somehow...**Go figure!**

I head downstairs again with my water bottle, sipping and pondering, as I go into another round of disablement, going nowhere, slowly, uncomfortably, not knowing why. This has happened before, more than twice. Each time just before a major blow or change in my life cycle, experience or situation. In the days leading up to and including this episode, I feel my breath so faintly that it could stop without me knowing. I feel I need to make a conscious effort to breathe all the way into my body as if it won't touch me otherwise. My breath is now on manual, auto is not currently available. I wonder.... What is this bout of insanity about? **What is about to hit or happen to me that will change my mind or course trajectory... again?**

The first two times this happened to me was in the year leading up to my mother-in-law's passing. Our beautiful fairy Grandma was only 54, and we were not ready to let her go so soon, nor would we be now either. Her passing, 5 days after she arrived in Australia for my 40th birthday, was a shock but not a surprise. I had already seen her lifeless body on her life-after-death bed in several dreams leading up to this moment. I worry when I see people I love deceased, before it happens. I did not know when exactly she would depart, or what to do with this information at the time. I miss you Janet xxx

The next couple of times I felt this experience take over me was in the year leading up to my marriage breakup. One of these times, we were camping in Iluka. This time shook me particularly hard. The campsite was pitch black. There was nowhere to go that felt any better than staying put, lying still in the fetal position, staring into the night through the mesh tent windows, trying to get my bearings and keep my heart at a calm rate. I did not want to awaken or panic my family as I needed to focus on my own calm and safety. This has so far been a lone journey, and I am glad. I don't think

I could cope with anyone watching me go through this or trying to help me without having experienced this themselves. They will not understand the helplessness and need for uninterrupted space until I fall asleep and snap out of it.

Staring into the darkness has me feeling smothered and claustrophobic. Staying in a well-lit room has me feeling trapped in the light, too much light to handle. This has not been in my experience by day. I can't even think myself into this situation by day, or even as I head off and lay in bed, drifting off to sleep. It hits me in my sleep, slaps me awake and drags me full-on into it. It is a sudden happening that has control over me. Thinking about it does not make it manifest.

This is an extremely powerful effect of a virtual reality that has increased in length astronomically. This last time, I was held in this illusion of spaceless-ness for two hours before falling asleep and waking up 20 minutes later, slap back in it. **NOOOOOOO!**

After this time check, I did not want to look at my phone again. I just concentrated on getting the right balance of dark and light awareness into my body, so I could settle my nervous system enough to nod off. I don't know how to get on top of this right now. It doesn't fade away while I am awake. I eventually fall asleep, and when I wake up, I'm good as gold. I don't worry about where or when it might happen again. However, I am suddenly weary of where I stay overnight. I can't predict it, and I don't feel it coming. It just arrives and wakes me up into it. **Aaaaargh!**

I wonder what I am doing or not doing that brings this on? Or, what is coming my way that it might be preparing me for? The episode I had just before this one was a few days before my almost 18-year-old daughter flew from my nest to her dads in NZ to start Uni. Perhaps this was the trigger for my feelings of helplessness at that time. It may be my soul's tough-love way of making me face more dark and light, to let go of evermore fear of past conditioning and future reconditioning.

All this, so I can move forward more freely, as an authentic seed of my original soul star, in full expression, without hesitation. Perhaps it's an intense and exaggerated expression of the light and dark particles in my body, putting on a shakey show. **Far out!**

We were staying at a friend's in Tyalgum, just after Christmas 2020. I was sleeping on a mattress on the floor. The kids were asleep together in the bed. I like my space, so I opted for the mattress on my own. I'm sensitive to energy, and I dream a lot, sometimes attempting to yell myself awake and out of the tortures of my nightmares. My daughter does the same.

This time in Tyalgum, I woke to find myself in a panic, on my hands and knees on the floor, desperately trying to feel my way out of complete darkness and into just enough light to know where I was, to feel grounded. This was not a quick process, as I collected my thoughts about the room I was sleeping in, the layout, and the closest light source I could possibly find my way to ASAP! When I woke, I was a few metres from where I had been sleeping. I felt the large curtains that hung over the external French-style doors and scrambled to find a gap between them, to hopefully let some light in. To my dismay and distress, there was none! The beautiful countryside we were privileged to be invited into and welcomed by, was blacked out completely.

And so, another wave of panic came over me. I had to think quickly and calmly. Where would I go next for just a little bit of light, to hold me and love me back to a state of serenity? The en-suite bathroom was my next stop, again on all fours. I found it less intense being down low in complete darkness, for some reason. I thought about the torchlight on my phone, but I would need to find my way to it first. It all came together in a few long minutes after. I sat on the closed toilet seat, wondering what on Earth to do with myself next.

Luckily most of my encounters were only a few hours away from the morning light, and that comforted me somewhat. It was still most unhelpful in those drawn-out moments of uncertainty and madness. It would have scared me more if I knew I was facing further into the hours of darkness, though. You can't plan your exit from these nighttime terrors. You don't know when they will hit or where you will be. It makes me wonder how many other Souls suffer from this experience and how it affects their overall life.

It has just come to my bedside attention that the realities of dark and light are not too dissimilar. The energy of life in this form we find ourselves extending into may be no different to that of the after-life or the lives we go to once we shoot for the stars again. I lay in wonder if my empathic self is making conscious connections to all that ever was and is to be, by experiencing them in real-time, as one and the same, feeling the negative vibes of dark and light at the same time. Am I finding myself more present than I am clearly comfortable with? There seems to be an energy in the darkness of night that randomly holds me in its grip, but why? Am I supposed to take direct notice of something in particular? The atmosphere feels humid, fully loaded and yet empty at the same time. I seem to find myself facing polarised realities simultaneously, quite a lot. **Ho hum!**

Perhaps what I'm experiencing is my soul expanding my ability to feel the power of high (conscious awareness) and low (unhealed parts) frequency quantum energy and magnifying the pressure in my body between the two. **Oh great!!**

It seems that with every new level of understanding comes a new level of ideas and reality to explore. As with everything that I do not have exact answers to, I have to let it go...for now. A student of the Universe can only lean closer, listen in and let go more, as the questions surrounding existence come up from perpetual and sometimes painful, personal experience. I wonder if the answers would come pouring in if I could just hold the space right? I'm working on it! Time will tell.

Sometimes all of our thoughts are misleading.... and it makes me wonder – Led Zeppelin

My soul tells me; **'I feel you. It's metaphysical, biological overload!'**

Soul Message

Expansion into all that is, as you can or cannot imagine, is a never-ending measure of all you could possibly experience, express and handle, on all levels of reality and being. Think energetically, spiritually and scientifically. Virtually anything you can think, imagine, sense, make up or create, tangibly or not, can offer many powerful teachings and truths. Taking you to extended states of awareness around your body, your mind, and beyond a typical human life is the nature of your greatest asset, your soul. Your human form struggles with the vastness of consciousness that puts you on the spot.

Big breath here! Your occasional states of helplessness are related to the retaining of your sliding past and the resistance to your ascending future. It is in more than the mind. It is energy in motion and emotion. Your expansive self is diving into the unknown. To accept and master a little more of every part of your being, her love for all life, and human potential. And so, we ask you to expand your awareness into your body, beyond the surface, to the multi-layered bodies that hinder your readiness and hold your resistance to further change in a heart lock. You will find your way out of this next maze in good time. Just like everything else you have come to know of the human condition, you will find better ways of coping until you break through barriers and build new boundaries on your way to self fullness. Have you called in for the wisdom of others yet? **Nope, didn't think so!**

Deeeeper! (Must be said in a high pitched voice, ok.)
Geese, Abigail and Amelia - Aristocats

19 – Wireless Beings

Wireless, energetic beings of light
Illuminating the Universe, with all of our might
Healing our species, reviving, restoring
Sharing our wisdom, gently mentoring

Being courageous, leading the way
Soul-sourced originals, creative at play
Living intuitively, encouraging fulfilment
Enlightening spirits, teaching contentment

Spreading awareness, conscious and pure
Activating every energy core
Raising vibration, beyond limitation
Lovingly nurturing the whole of creation

Gracefully evolving, soaring above
Joyous and driven to circulate love
Living in harmony, with all that you be
Grateful and worthy, balanced and free

Close Encounters

February 2020, I awoke with a vision in my mind's eye. It was an imprint of a transparent, glassy-looking, sacred geometric shaped spaceship hovering above my bed. My body was filled with super-charged electrical energy like it was pumping boiling blood through my veins until it slowed to a simmer on waking fully. There was no heat present, just high powered movement of energy, reacting as it hit and merged with my dense form. It felt as if I had been beamed back into my room from a distant galaxy, transported first-class at the speed of timeless light. The weight on my chest was intense with the power of much more consciousness than I have ever been privileged to hold. It was only temporary, as usual, as I returned to my solid form with only slightly more awareness than I went to bed with the night before. This was not the first time an unidentified flying object had ubered me around without my human consent. Something was changing. Something new was up! I just thought that **this human experience I am in may not be my main life or priority form of existence. Hmmmm?**

Perhaps my consciousness in this incarnation needs to catch up with the rest of the me's, that delve and dive deep into other realms.

Where do you go?

I wanna know... my lovely - No Mercy

Since this experience, I have had a metal tapping/clicking sound around my right ear. It does not feel like it is coming from inside my ear canal, but it is definitely connected to me somehow. It's quite random and sometimes comes when I feel I am being watched or monitored. I tried to work it out, but it does not happen every time I expect it. I have observed it, thinking maybe it is my earrings, wet hair or holding my head a certain way, wax or the need to make my ears pop, but nothing has been obvious or consistent. Sometimes it doesn't happen for days or weeks. This week, it has been all on! I have also felt like my inner ear was an antenna or GPS scanning for information.

Soul Message - 12 September 2021

For many, the collective consciousness moves beyond the spiritual realm and into the galactic space. We have reached out to many of you for expanded awareness for longer than you can imagine. And so here we all now sit, together in presence, to learn from each other, every one a student and every one a teacher. You are relaying information of the human experience back to your source points and us returning the favour, connecting dots of your resident constellations in many previous and concurrent existences. It is a slow process for some, it seems. While this is of no consequence to the energy of your original source, the human form and its incarnate energy body favour an experience of shifting and shaping out of the old and into the new at a greater rate of less knarly knots.

It's life Jim...but not as we know it – The Firm

May 2021 – An interesting morning message arrives - The consciousness of humanity is a work in progress. This means that humanity's work is in progress. The light work that is being carried out is gaining traction against dark forces and integrating with it, not so slowly anymore. Some wonder when your dimension will be infiltrated with Alien aircraft, technology, beings and species. For many, this reality is miles away, and for others, it is here already and has been in their experience for eons. You have seen the memes of one light body amongst the fighters defending cause and effect. You have seen the gradual results of holding your light dearly, even in times of pain. This is proof that your homecoming is, in fact, becoming a greater light-bearing pillar of support. Holding spaces of light becomes easier as you choose a path that recognizes truth, releases fear, and rises above your human resistance, embracing all that is in this entire non-sensical existence.

As the bodies of light increase in numbers and awareness, the third-dimensional realities become less cumbersome. You notice your mind questions the source of this information. You are still learning to let us in. Trusting is your challenge. Trust is where and what you need to restore your power.

Human beings are standing in as themselves more, standing up for themselves and standing out with their voice and views. More humans are considering how they are being, choosing to focus on living from and with their own light in all that matters. Strengthening abilities, capabilities and igniting their potential, for it is this potential in each individual that will add a touch of gold to silver linings.

We have made sufficient up-close and personal contact with you to anchor a strong connection and implant energetically wired lines of communication around you in your field so that we may communicate our thoughts, forms and information to you without overloading and exhausting your maturing inner human space. We have the blessing of your soul to do this. However, you may be released from your connection with us at any time by avoiding our calls for your attention, waving you to slow down for a new and improved galactic experience. Your Soul has always been associated with us here. It is merely the powerful human psyche you hold that is clinging to its rebellious nature, ha ha!

We love you and appreciate that you now, finally, give your time to writing and deepening human knowledge and experience through your unique channel. You are not alone, so you must find your team of Galactic Leaders, Spiritual Warriors and Sages. You got this! Infinitely yours... (**I will share more in my next writing adventure!**)

19 – Wireless Beings

This desirable new energy is expected to serve deeper levels of peace, calm and wisdom into your personal fields to stay. Be steady on your course, and you will not be let down. Be aware of the darkness you run from and the light you run into. Each will have consequences to navigate and neutralise as you decide how to face each, with your readiness for truth.

Breathe deep into your body when you concentrate on the image of the **Galactic Self** (back cover of this book). Allow this symbol to project its frequency upon you, into you, empowering the very Soul that you are, to come forward and magnify if you can handle it in this moment. Settle into this space. You can call it home if it speaks to you as such. Feel the presence of your undertones and overtones calling you into order amongst the chaos of extreme and diverse possible realities. Observe the sensations as your body reacts and responds to distant memories of your most original energy source. Feel into this divine connection as it retrains you to embody and express attributes of your original points of creation. Know that you are being held in spaces that support this human extension of your self.

We are beginning to break free from the main stream of anything and everything. Welcome this feeling of power and light into your presence daily. In every sense of the words, lighten up. It will recharge your being and top up your cups with the essence of your whole self. You will soon see the love at the end of your proverbial tunnels.

Humanity is recognizing the growing call out for standing amongst the collective stars as a one of a celestial kind. Answer your sacred, private calls. This is one of them!

It's like a journey I just don't have a map for!
Savage Garden

20 – Happy Anniversary

To my beautiful husband, my partner in life
I feel honoured and blessed to be your wife
You are gentle and kind, loving and caring
Who would have thought of the two of us paring?

Our journey together is not always logical
I am intuitive, you are methodical
Sometimes we make headway, some days we backtrack
Sometimes we start new, or need to mend cracks

Our relationship's seen unpredictable times
We've had to fall down, then get up and climb
You're one of a kind, honest and sharing
When I look around, there's just no comparing

10 years of marriage and 19 together
Working things out, we're in this forever
Living and loving, laughing til sore
Closing the old, opening new doors

Enjoying our babies, half you and half me
Playing together, learning to see
That we have only now to experience and be
So let's keep life simple, curious and free

Very Important Date

September 1989, my new date arrives to pick me up for the first time. I am spotting hash oil on tin foil in my bedroom and inhaling it through a rolled up five dollar bill. A semi-regular occurrence on top of my Benson and Hedges cigarettes, LSD trips and copious amounts of beer, brandy & dry and vodka, lime and lemonade. These were my coping mechanisms for a severe lack of self-love and acceptance. The suppression of my childhood traumas, the pressure of expectation and denied entry to the seeds of life that I really wanted to bloom from drove me to reside within my darker side.

I did not expect this young man to stick around for long. He was beautiful, with the hugest blue eyes I had ever seen, lashes to match and a confident and gentle temperament. He was surely not a match for my unworthy, messed up self. ☹ I was wrong. Physical attraction is an interesting thing. We often put our biological needs at the top of our daily priorities. That's where I believe we stayed through most of our years together. I also had several 'normal' jobs before our children were born, which kept him around a little longer, lol. While I was dealing with insecurity and lack of self-worth, I believe he was dealing with avoidance of all the kind of yucky stuff that my soul was about to drag me deep into. This is just my opinion, of course, but that **physical attraction, when played right, makes all the pain go away....right?**

'Cause it's a bitter, sweet... sym phony, that's liife!
– The Verve

In 1998, I skipped down the aisle, like a lamb in Spring, to be his bride anyway. With my dad lovingly on my arm, Wet Wet Wet's version of Love Is All Around delightfully played my tones. This was my song, not my ex hubby to be's, just mine, and it still is.

I feel it in my fingers....I feel it in my toes – Wet Wet Wet

Our life was filled with love and lessons the same as any other relationship, until one day, we could no longer relate. I used to think that you only got divorced because you hated each other, you were never meant to be, or someone made a wrong move that compromised your connection. Sometimes, it may come to those things, but it's really all about incompatibility. You read the signs and either follow them to a more harmonious individual path, or you ignore them and try to make each other sit, stay and be your ideal partner just so everything in your garden can appear rosy. It's quite hilarious to me now. I liken it to two totally different species of animals trying to cohabitate smoothly and effectively when their basic functional needs and wants are incomparable.

Laughing all the way, ha, ha, ha!...not laughing ☹

In 2013, I could feel NZ calling, so we planned a trip back to catch up with all of our family. I was looking forward to it. On top of that, I had this deep excitement that something big would happen on my return. It did! Separation and divorce were in the making, although I was still unsure why. My soul was clearly in support of this change of direction, but my semi-detached human was not.

It seemed that my husband's idea of moving back to NZ was confused with my clear intent to visit only. As the energy of differences began to frustrate us, we let go of each other a little more each day, reaching inside and out for guidance and resolve. It was unclear for me as I was not officially aware of the timing or nature of his close encounters or reconnection with the third of our kind until after the fact. Usual story, right? That's communication challenges for you. I guess we spoke different languages.

Haere ra husband! (The Queen's wave here)

I still didn't believe that he would cut me off so abruptly, so quickly. After all, he was the nice one of the two of us. The funny thing is, due to my strong need for variety in almost every way, I used to joke that it was amazing that he was still around and that I had settled in with him for the long haul. I didn't get the last laugh there either. Dammit! It was a quick clean cut for him, but it left a soiled wound in my heart and identity.

I loved being a wife. Booo hoo hoo ☹

You see, I fell in love with a man who had already written his name in the stars next to someone else's. Although, for several years, my clairvoyance had been showing me them together, I did not know how to stop it from happening. I was not prepared to let that insecurity get the better of me. The blessing in disguise eventually revealed itself. After our separation, I realised that we were so uncomfortable attempting to walk our own paths together that we found ourselves challenged with each other's ways of getting to where our hearts lay waiting, whether there was a third party involved or not. I thank goodness for that third party now. Without her, I would not be free to be me. **Hallelujah! Happy families.** 😊

Thank you, next! – Ariana Grande

Sadly, the two of us had hidden many aspects of ourselves from each other so as not to cause conflict. Aspects, dreams, desires, wants and needs that we felt like we needed permission from each other to investigate and participate in. In all areas of life, variety and spontaneity were super high on my Souls needs. This conflicted with his soul's needs for certainty and stability, leading us astray from our greatest personal values. Our ways of thinking, being and doing were very different, even though we loved similar things too and had lots of belly laughs. I had become highly sensitive and intuitive to energy and spirit. He was steadfast in all that was logical, practical, methodical, reasonable, linear and 'common' sense. My personal awareness has led me to see that a common thread of sense is not always best or helpful, and certainly not for me.

Although all great attributes, I could feel myself drifting from these popular dimensions of reality. It felt like I fitted better in this new, increasing space of diversity.

I, I, I ,I ,I ,I feel something sooo wrong... doing the right thing – One Republic

I could sense intolerance building up in my husband towards me, as the desire for personal transformation took a stronghold on me, and he could no longer see any kind of certainty in our future together. It was not a 'normal' way of life calling me. I was random and spontaneous, overactive and unpredictable. What a nightmare for a typically grounded partner (BIG eyes here). I was also his distraction until 'they' could meet again. He was my distraction from the being I was afraid would be too much for him, too much for me and too much for anyone I loved. And so, I had to face that being, the one of intense light disguised as darkness, that I was afraid of because she was charging towards me, challenging my naive mind, ready, steady go! That being wanted a different life for herself and her children. She was going to show me the way. The weakest link in my consciousness had now been removed from my illusionary possession. I am not talking about the person, just the unreal idea that this person was aligned with my destiny and going to support my every move forever. You may be familiar with this example too.

In the early days, our ideas of a future together did not look the same. I appeared more risky. Some of his friends did not like me very much either, and they made it obvious. I don't know if it was the nose piercing and tiny tattoo on my ankle (big things back then), my leather and lace, or just my high-on-life overactive self. To be fair, I don't blame them. He was more calculated and conscientious than me. Everyone loved him. It was a battle of wills that took us a step back from each other as often as we moved forward together. Mentally, emotionally and spiritually, we were not on the same page. **Good to know that now, hey?**

I still loved him. So in one of these, could have been better times, I had a momentary glimpse of him in the future. He was right in front of me when I watched him in silence. I did not recognise him so much as the love of my life anymore. For a brief few moments, I was stunned, as these words came to me: 'By the time he notices who you are, your interest in being beside him will be long gone. You will no longer be so besotted with him.' I knew this was for the best, but I had no idea why. I snapped out of it and tried to imagine it actually happening. I believed it would. Even with the signs of incompatibility right in front of us, we humans still prefer to see something else, anything but the end of the road.

Again, I still loved him. I'm pleased to say that I now know the difference between loving someone and being in love with them. It's common for at least one partner to not love themselves and so, be unable to love the other in their entirety. I accept things now about each of us that I once couldn't have. This was my road of choice, and it meant that I was going to go it alone for a while, actually a long while, while I worked it all out. **Big sigh!**

I hadn't been loving life my own way fully, and clearly, neither had he. Now on my own with the little ones, it was tough, and I was a rough diamond for sure. Grumping and growling through the cavity of my broken heart, trying to find a way out of the hurt, a way to be ok with it all. Unable to counsel or communicate with the love that left my life, I had no option but to wade through the mass of my own confusion by myself. He had a new life, one without me in it. It seemed he was happy and wanted to forget about me altogether. It became clear on our last interaction, just before he left, when my tears were interrupted by a palm in the air and his voice telling me he was not emotionally there. Luckily, I was pretty quick to realise he was not hi-fiving me, **haha (not funny at the time).**

I made a decision not to fight about anything. Whatever he wanted, he could have. I did not go into that relationship to be a kept woman, although he may have thought so. I did not have greed on my mind or hatred in my heart towards him, only sadness. I knew that I could love him, no matter whether we had a roof over our head or a bite to eat. Clearly, he was not of the same frame of heart and mind, though he did support me financially, as the main carer of our children, without any request from me. Thanks to this man meeting with his match, I was also left to be me in my own world, without interference from him and his expectations. All his needs were being taken care of elsewhere, so I gradually and gratefully accepted this and let him go too.

I eventually reunited with my humorous spirit, who turned my choice of unwavering acceptance into a lesson of pure delight, comedy and solid gold. Every time something came up with this man that opposed my own ideals, I would get angry, furious actually! ***I would stomp around (privately, of course) like Rumplestiltskin, growl loudly into a pillow and fall dramatically into a heap, sobbing helplessly, as if it was the end of my ego's world.*** After the tsunami of emotion had made it out, I would get a glimpse of myself from outside of my body. The shock of my behaviour would suddenly push my funny button, and off I would go, into the land of hilarity, laughing madly at my own ridiculousness, insecurities and inability to deal with them maturely.

At this stage, I would consider how far I had come with self-mastery and how far I was prepared to go. Little did I know at the beginning that this journey was going to be a long one for this crazy, curious soul!

The kids and I like to keep it light by referring to my eccentricities as *o.t.b.t, over the bl—dy top, ha ha.* It takes away the pressure and pain that being too serious, dramatic and victimised lays in concrete. And so we get raw (mostly me), we stay real (mostly them), we laugh and let go. This process allows the love within us to expand, prevail and endure. It can be contagious for anyone consciously caught in the web that lies in truth. Add the presence of chocolate, and nobody gets hurt much at all. **YAY!**

Soul Message

Emotional intelligence sits in the space between being emotionally unavailable and emotionally overcharged. It is a trait of the human being to take a side of duality and protect it with all they have invested in it. This includes the contents they wish to avoid and the perceived achievements they hope to replace them with by not entering the dark whole of emotional value. You have been dealing with your own battle of resistance between these two states. Harmony, resolve, and forward movement becomes available when the overcharged victim leaves the drama for the stage and the fighting for the mat. When the one lacking emotion allows presence and vulnerability to flow with honesty, in and out of their body freely. Each can grieve and heal more smoothly in unison.

The energy field that contained set relationship dynamics can now close and dissolve with ease. It is difficult to bypass the grieving state of all perceived ideas and unfulfilled expectations of self and others and go straight into complete happiness elsewhere, without acceptance and letting go. Avoidance, judgement and blame are ticking truth bombs, with fading best-before dates. The choice is yours to disarm them intentionally or wait for them to explode! Choosing the latter will attract challenges to the physical body and show signs of dis-ease, as inner disharmony reminds you of the disturbances you have chosen not to approach, heart on. This can generate a slow release of pain-filled human experience on any and every level of being, as you opt for the by-pass at all costs.

This level of maturity is not prevalent in the awareness of partnerships changing their form of contact and relating. This behaviour keeps them polar opposite to the core energy of their soul's centre, as they plod along in a predictable, repetitive, kind of manner, with limited re-creativity and renewal. The quality of your experience in the material world will be relative to your love, respect, appreciation and joy for and within what most deem as immaterial, the invisible energy of quantum loving magic. Avoidance disregards the intangible as if it is less notice-worthy. Even if the material side of someone's life appears to be solid, know that their personal experience in it will most likely be filled with hidden private challenges to maintain and keep it so. How you play your hand on healing the less understood as much as the obvious will determine what life deals you in return. You will have all you like once you integrate this alternative awareness of reality into your reality. **Fascinating!**

Here's a thought for you to ponder. If in future you plan to live in a little house, share a little bedroom, sleep in a little bed and wake up next to the same person for the rest of your life, you might want to be pretty sure you make a good match, that you are compatible on mental, emotional and spiritual levels as well. Observe behaviours closely and notice if you both have a deep sense of understanding, acceptance and care for each other in all states of being. Check your incompatibilities for deal-breakers and follow the signs, to your way out peacefully and respectfully. Recognise if you are just tolerating certain parts of them while you work on changing them for what you think is their own good. This strategy doesn't work too well.

Me -*Oh-kaaay, thanks for the retrospective wisdom, smart soul!* (eye roll and meh emoji here)

Soul Message Continued

Your soul waits for you at the edge of everything you know. It is one step ahead of your current reality and beckons you to explore the unknown. You are part of the unknown. With your soul in alignment, you can climb up over the edge to reach greater heights of awareness and expand your experiences. It is only your mind that interprets the edge as a place to be wary of, in case you fall over it. Fear not. The edge is above you. Whatever you see is what you get.

So... why... don't... you... turn me loose?...

I gotta do it my way...or no way at all! Loverboy

21 – Self Love

Being real, being true
Being Beautiful Powerful You
Loving your self, loving your skills
Unique, original, no drama or frills

Leading the way, having your say
Singing your voice to work and play
Going hard out and then not at all
Increasing momentum, balancing falls
Keeping head up, spirit and chin
Daring to be seen, comfy in your skin

21 – Self Love

Nothing Sweet About Me

Gabriella Cilmi

June 2018 - As I write in this moment, I do not have the pieces of my life all together. Sometimes I feel whole, at one with who I am and am not, and sometimes I don't. I have accepted this as a challenge of the human lifetime. I am supported by my dear soul, one tiny, huge spirit of adventure, in a Universe of conscious and spiritual awakening. Today, as I gaze around my colourful bedroom, I am at peace with my journey, at ease with my human self, and in love with the peacefulness I have created thus far. These magical words whisper to me, and I take note.

Soul Message

'As you let go of the need to control everything, you gain the ability to orchestrate anything. Your days of carrying your energy like an armed force become less as your soul steps you into the dance of your heart's beats, the harmonious symphony behind the curtain of your doubts and fears. You, the conductor of this energy, are the leader of your favourite means and melodies to beginnings and ends.

Me

Still, I am cleaning and housekeeping to pay the bills. I feel like Cinderella, dressed in well-worn gym gear, always sweaty and feeling dirty. My unique difference is that I am my own wicked step mother and annoying step sister too. Holding myself there, chained to the cleaning up of my life, totally responsible for keeping every area of space I inhabit clear, free of what lurks, clutters, numbs, muddies and clouds my thinking, feelings, words and actions. 100% accountable, alone. **No way Jose'!**

I have been a hermit in hiding, holding out on all the gifts that have come through to me, too terrified to unleash my whole self on anyone, let alone many. **Hilarious! Who do I think I am?** I have worried about what other people might think or say about me. Their non-acceptance and being seen to suck or be too great at anything for too long. It's a no-win situation! Sticks and stones may break our bones, but why do names hurt deeply too?

Watch what you say.... or they'll be calling you radical... - Supertramp

So here I am, speaking, writing, healing myself to free my Soul, taking the leash off my human self and allowing her to be guided by the intensity of her soul's in-tense voice. **Hoo... jolly... raaah!**

BUT...

The world outside looks so un...kiiind

So I'm counting on yooou.....to carry me through

Oh, give me the beat... to free my soul...Doobie Brothers

Soul message continued

When you compare yourself with others, you look to them for what they think you should do, what you should have and how you should be and behave to be an acceptable, loved and accomplished member of society. If you follow the energy of someone else's dream, life and style, you will be missing your own unique magic, and settling on being another version of the same creature. How sad for humanity that they would miss out on your marvel and magnificence because you think others have got what it takes, and you don't. Is this what you wish for others? Your children? I think not!

How about we choose you a different tune, and...

Let your love flow... like a mountain stream and let your love grow...with the smallest of (your) dreams and let your love show....Bellamy Brothers

22 – Wish You Were Here

To our beautiful Dad, you've left us too soon
Now you're taking your place, with the sun and the moon
Where I shall think of you, each day and night
Inspiring me to raise my vibe to new heights
Our hearts are wide open, they've cracked with grief
Our minds are confused, we're in disbelief

We're hurt, and we cry, the pain is too real
That time ran out for you to heal
You're a powerful man Dad, right to this end
We have loads of kisses and with you, we'll send
I miss you already my precious Dad
Devastated and wishing that more time we had

To chitchat and hug, make memories and live
To share our stories, receive and give
Where have you gone Dad, and will you be back?
With your butt-kicking love to keep us on track
Thank you for blessing my life with your presence
Shining your light, gifting your essence

I hope you're at peace Dad. Please come visit me
From your place among stars, the earth and the sea
My door's always open, wherever you are
I'm sorry I can't touch you, I feel so afar
Your life's not been peaches and cream all the way
I wish you'd felt better, I want you to stay

Sometimes life sucks Dad. This is one of those times
Please forgive my sad soul as it rants and it rhymes
'I'm full of 'what ifs' Dad, emptiness too
But I have so much praise, as your credit is due
I feel rough Dad. It's tough…raw and unreal
Vulnerable, fragile, inconsolable, I feel

Please send me a message. I'll wait in my heart
To see through the veil where no one departs
I'm heavy and gutted, down but not out
The love that you are still drifts and stands out
I hope your soul's free Dad, it soars and it flys
As we lay with your body and say last goodbyes

We're not done with you yet, Dad. We'll forget you never
The seeds that you've planted will nourish us forever
Is it too much to ask, Dad, for a little more time?
Will you hear our whispers through spirits grape vine?

I'm Sorry for your loss Dad
Please forgive me for not being there
Thank you for being so Beautiful and Powerful
I love you xxx Tash

Bye Dad

When I learned my dad was seriously unwell in 2019, I knew he was suffering from unhealed childhood trauma, plus everything that came after that too. I knew Dad was severely deficient in feeling the love he needed for his body to thrive. I'm not sure everyone will see it that way.

When my dad passed away in NZ in October 2021, I was in Australia and unable to be with him in person due to travel restrictions. My mum sent me the card they had made for his funeral service. It was a great shot of dad on the cover. He looked beautiful and powerful. But, when I looked into his eyes, I saw the man I was afraid of while growing up. Inside the cover, the older looking version of my dad, although well worn, was the gentler, softer man he became. This was the man that I felt deep sadness for as I grew to love and admire him greatly over his last decade or two. I feel at peace with the sense that Dad left knowing he found his place back in my heart, just as I had in his.

Arohanui Dad xxx

For several years as a young adult, I had a recurring dream that I was at the edge of the ocean, watching countless people and animals, mostly horses, flounder about, trying desperately to keep their heads above water. My dad was the main character in this dream. I would swim out to save him and haul him back into land, only to find him back out there, struggling to tread water again, as I scurried to rescue other family members and strangers. I have wondered since the recent unfoldings if my attempts to pull Dad from the main body of energy that most people float their lives upon was symbolic of my desires to help my dad to wellness, with a more holistic and natural approach than the common space he was offered and held unsuccessfully in. I wondered too if my dad's going out to that main body of powerful energy was his soul's choice and none of my business.

Perhaps my continuous laps to save him in my dreams would be enough to anchor energetically, emotionally and spiritually into my own awareness that Dad felt my efforts and knew how much I loved and supported him as unconditionally as I was showing him face to face. I did my best in my dreams and real-time, and so did Dad. That is all we can expect from ourselves and others. I still wish he was here and we could try something new for him. I miss the humour in his character, and I feel his cheeky ways in me too.

Don't worry.......about a thing... cause every little thing's...gonna be all right

...This is my message to yooou - Bob Marley (Dad's service commencing music)

Tonight as my head hits the pillow, I feel a warm energy enter my field and sit just beneath my skin. I sense my heart beating in my throat and feel emotions rising in my abdomen. I ask if this feeling is mine or someone else's. I see my dad clairvoyantly, and I chat with him telepathically. He is okay. He does not stay with me long. I recall the last video Messenger conversation I had with him about trying alternative healing and treatments. I wish I had been there to support him back into wellness. Tonight I am sad that the last two years of Dad's life were unpleasant for him. **Dad deserved better xxx.**

Lean on me...when you're not strong....and I'll be your friend – Bill Withers

(Dad's recessional music)

I knew several years ago that Dad wouldn't be here when my book came out. It's probably the biggest reason for my enduring resistance to publishing it. It's pretty heavy stuff. Not for everyone.

One of these kids... is not... like the others – Sesame Street

Two weeks after Dad slipped away, I had the urge to draw what appears to be a light-language style of writing.

When I try to interpret this message, my heart rate becomes more noticeable, and the sound heats my body, sending warm shivers right through me. The energy of this message plays on my heart, tugging at strings of sadness and pain. This feels like a language of light, love and healing magic. It unlocks melancholy and uncried tears. I felt strong in its initial presence, and now, as the walls come down, *I feel weak in the*

presence of its beauty (lyrics from Alison Moyet). I feel a feminine being, beautiful and powerful, gently swaying and playing with the energy of love around her, around me and striking a symphony of chords within my physical body. I feel my spirit rise to the top of my priorities. I love her subtle supporting style...turns out she is me. And then another energetic Messenger joins us.

Soul and Friends, Message

We would like to relay the message to keep your chin and heart rate up with all the love you can muster at this time. The processing of loss is hard, but as you see, it is becoming quicker and easier for you. Do not judge yourself for this. This is expansive conscious being. This message aims to rebalance you in a moment, to return you to a state of acceptance along with the joy of opposing realities you experience. This message serves to guide your energy to dance around your body again while you still have much life left in it. This light message whispers, come back home, home to your whole self, the one that is not fragmented with grief and trauma, the one that is not high on false positives either. Come home to the one that remains and returns to high vibrations as the processing of loss ushers you back to the seat of your beautiful, powerful soul.

You are opening, lightening, freeing yourself from unnecessary structures of control, including the grid of human death. Extreme depths of this grid can hinder your ability to remain grounded and live one's own remaining life joyously. You are dealing with the process of releasing grief from your close family, as well as your own. They will find themselves doing the same for you too. It is a sign of your bonds and love for each other. Your absence from their physical vicinity makes the energy between you build. And like a giant snowball rolled towards you from such a distance, it feels like it could knock you for a six.

When you feel that your best or only form of existence relies on what you lost, the person you loved and wanted to keep loving, the place you found your most joy in or the thing that juiced you up, then you best face that idea and dismantle it. When you have no regrets about your connection with the person, no anger or frustration at yourself for not trying hard enough, you will have no neediness to make amends or have one more chance to say sorry, thank you or goodbye. You won't fall victim to the state of sadness that is stricken with guilt and shame. The healing process is what happens as you accept that the suffering was not of your doing, and it is out of your control to change. This is where you find peace, even if it feels like your world has ended.

I never meant to cause you any sorrow...

I only wanted to see you laughing... in the purple rain – Prince

The beginning of a healing journey requires you to face all the bad things you feel happened to you, the sad and hurtful, shameful things done by yourself and others. The final stage or closure comes when you find all the good things, the love and care you expressed, the fun, joy and precious moments of acceptance. Together, the reconciliation of what you once deemed good and bad puts your emotions into neutral and your nervous system on lighter duties. From there, you can drive forward, free to recall and remember, experience and express, without encumbering vibrations messing with your mood and motivation.

Much love to you xxx

Conclusion

It's not easy being a multi-dimensional human being. Our thoughts, feelings and experiences can get muddled up in the collective field with everyone elses. Perhaps we are not so different after all. Pay close attention to the voice of your own soul through introspection, intuition and self-care. Accept and embrace your unique journey to bring your deepest loves and potential to life. No matter how slow or unusual it may seem, you will find your way to those who can relate as you learn how to relate to yourself. Form a deep relationship with ALL that you are, and true beauty and power will become you.

Contrary to the popular desires of Star Seeds and the sense of not belonging here, I do not feel myself to be like E.T, desperate to call and find my way home. I love it here...most of the time. It is just that I needed to find my personal space amongst all available possibilities and add some of my own. I give the intent that you too may find your way to the place that suits you best here. It's more the optical illusions I recognise in this material world that my soul does not wish to comply with or feel compelled to take part in. I am also aware that I need to be careful what I ask for. There are hidden agendas and gems that my human wants cannot navigate or effectively receive on their own. Universal laws contain algorithms that you cannot necessarily account for in your human manifestation techniques toolbox. I must listen to the voice of my soul as she vibrates the energy of her dreams through my heart. Anything out of alignment with that will not come close to me.

Taking a trip to your heart centre is like taking a journey to the centre of the Earth, where the core of essential being is protected by layers of natural wonders and wells. However, not everyone will want to visit these discomfort zones. My human needs are not on the same list as my soul's. If I am asking for anything, it will only arrive if its energy is in alignment with my goodness and grace.

I'd love this book to nudge you into the sense of your own soul. To release tears of joy and sadness as you recognise your history and acknowledge your unhealed human experiences, turning a colourful past into a rainbow of self-centred support for a creative and brighter future.

Right now... I'm in a state of mind...I wanna be in like, all the time

...***No tears left to cry...*** – Ariana Grande

The voice of your soul whispers to you all the time. Its purpose is to remind you of the joys you can gain on this journey of human experience. See the difficult times as a ripe environment to take charge and move through obstacles. You will regain personal power and the energy to create your ideal life. You will form a stronger sense of self, empowered by your own confidence, direction, support and growing capabilities. Share your talents gracefully and encourage others to do the same.

Be Beautiful, Be Powerful, Be You. Wishing you love and magic always, Natasha xxx

Acknowledgements

I'd like to say a huge THANK YOU to Emily Gowor for her patience and all her wonderful publishing tools that have helped me bring my book into the light. I purchased my package in 2017, and well....that was a while ago, lol. Thanks a million, Em. Your ability to hold space, stay focused and know exactly what to do next is impressive. I admire you. Thanks too for the butt-kicking emoji that kicked my final copy into action. Love it! xxx

Thank you to Rae Antony for reviewing my book and for sharing your honest and personal experience of it. It strengthened my faith in the purpose of Beautiful, Powerful You. I appreciate you xxx

Thank you to Aunty Sandy and Uncle Al for harassing me on my days off work, checking that I was doing what I was supposed to be doing and not faffing about aimlessly... I did not do that a lot! ...I did (eek). You can leave me alone now, haha! Thank you for your confidence in me to get this book done through my sweat and tears. You're the best fairy godmother and godfather I could have. I love you both xxx

Thank you to my talented teens.

Taegan, for loving and recreating my original piece of art for the front cover and some of the illustrations,

Acknowledgements

helping me choose colours and painting and photographing them perfectly for me from NZ. I'm so thrilled with it all and couldn't be more chuffed that you offered to do this for me and with me. Wish you were here for a huge hug. I love you, my sweetness xxx

Chad for creating a digital version of my original sketch for the back cover, with added oomph, for painting illustrations, and for designing and producing the whole cover digitally. You were easily the best person for the job. It's even better than I imagined. I love you, my darlingness xxx

Thank you to Nelson Eulalio for your professional feedback and support on our homemade book cover. Your advice was most valuable and appreciated xxx

Thank you to my five-year-old inner child for her patience and perseverance with my 52 year-old adult self, as I took my time in healing her experience and acknowledging the gifts in her soul and stories. I love you, little one xxx Natasha

About The Author

Natasha has had the urge to write ever since she was a child but always declined putting anything down on paper for fear of rejection and humiliation. Throughout her life, Natasha was in awe of Writers and Poets and is now grateful for her own writing abilities. Through her channelled writings, Natasha learned to acknowledge, accept and move on from her past. She learned to stop projecting too far into the future and live more of her life in the simplicity of the present moment. Since her writing began, Natasha has learned many things about her deeply caring soul's creative and intuitive abilities that she once denied and neglected. Her poetry and soul messages have taught Natasha to continue on a path of self-discovery and to treasure her connection to all things mystical and phenomenal. With the help of her fun-loving soul, Natasha loves to combine music and humour with her writings to lighten the energy and support the healing process. Natasha's abilities have recently extended to channelled art, and her next book is already in the making.

Love Note

My greatest mission as a parent has been to walk beside my kids, not over the top of them or in front of them. I cannot pretend to have all the best answers and right moves for their personal human experience and souls journey. The more effort I make to acknowledge, understand and support their every thought, feeling and desire, the more I see each of our potentials expand into free and creative states of being. The dreamer in me loves the magic of flexibility, full presence, increasing self awareness and total acceptance of what is true for each individual. I feel blessed that my kids have chosen to walk beside me and support my childhood dreams (the good ones) too 😊 In this project, they have held my hands and the space for me to express the voice of my soul. A beautiful and powerful intent has now come full circle 💖

Taegan Jones

Chad Jones

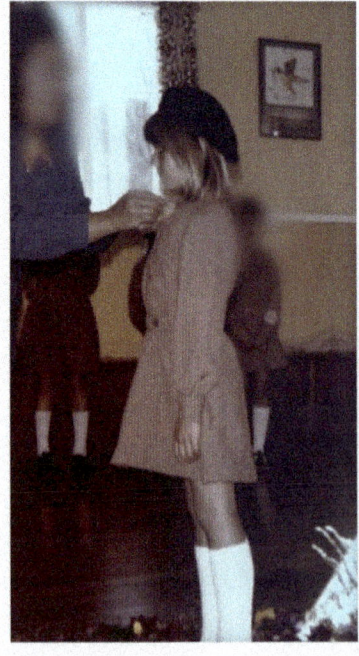

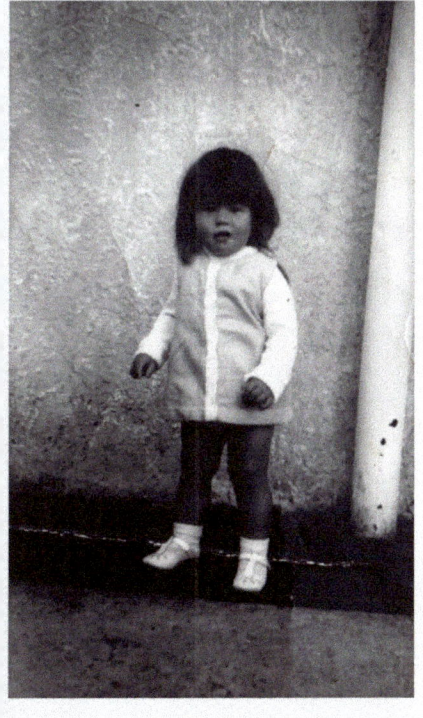

www.ingramcontent.com/pod-product-compliance
Ingram Content Group UK Ltd.
Pitfield, Milton Keynes, MK11 3LW, UK
UKHW061222180426
11947UKWH00026B/1967